50 World's Greatest Letters

CLASSICS

Reprint 2022

FiNGERPRINT! CLASSICS
An imprint of Prakash Books India Pvt. Ltd.

113/A, Darya Ganj,
New Delhi-110 002
Tel: (011) 2324 7062 – 65, Fax: (011) 2324 6975
Email: info@prakashbooks.com/sales@prakashbooks.com

facebook www.facebook.com/fingerprintpublishing
twitter www.twitter.com/FingerprintP
www.fingerprintpublishing.com

ISBN: 978 93 8777 983 9

Processed & printed in India

From the time of the quill and parchment, to that of the keyboard and computer screen, letters have been circulated for centuries. Ranging from handwritten to typewritten to printed, the letters exchanged are immense in quantity and rich in diversity. Men and women have made protestations of their love to each other through letters; citizens have written to their country's leaders to express their gratitude, and sometimes, also their concerns; parents have written to their children who were far away from home; and travellers have recorded their experiences in letters to friends and family. Permeated with letters about anything and everything, the epistolary world is filled with beautifully elegant and heartfelt words written by children, poets, novelists, scientists, ministers, presidents, artists, travellers, and even convicts.

With the advent of electronic communication, letters have become a rarity, a thing of the past, but their importance has not diminished. Along with constructing the reputation of its writer, a letter provides a window to the innermost recesses of the writer's mind, perhaps because it is personal, meant only for the eyes of its receiver. Who would have known that George Orwell was, actually, not happy with his phenomenal book, *1984*, perhaps because he had worked on it when he was sick? That Albert Einstein had been the catalyst behind starting America's nuclear race with Germany, would have remained a secret, if not for his letter to Franklin Roosevelt, America's then President. And would we not want to know what world leaders like George Bush and Winston Churchill talked about in their letters?

From simple letters that have declarations of love, words of advice, bursts of anger, and subtle insults, to letters of import, that have crystallized the moments of historical significance, fall back in love with letters through our edition that comprises fifty of the greatest letters ever written.

CONTENTS

I Can Do Everything Possible

Leonardo Da Vinci's letter[1] to Ludovico Sforza, written c. 1482

My Most Illustrious Lord,[2]

Having now sufficiently seen and considered the achievements of all those who count themselves masters and artificers of instruments of war, and having noted that the invention and performance of the said instruments is in no way different from that in common usage, I shall endeavour, while intending no discredit to anyone else, to make myself understood to Your Excellency for the purpose of unfolding to you my secrets, and thereafter offering them at your complete disposal, and when the time is right bringing

---

1 This letter was sent in the early 1480s. Its exact composition date is unknown.

2 Ludovico Sforza was the Duke of Milan. At the time, he was looking for mechanical engineers. Da Vinci drafted the letter according to his potential employer's needs, extolling his engineering abilities, and mentioned his painting skills only in passing.

into effective operation all those things which are in part briefly listed below:

1. I have plans for very light, strong and easily portable bridges with which to pursue and, on some occasions, flee the enemy, and others, sturdy and indestructible either by fire or in battle, easy and convenient to lift and place in position. Also means of burning and destroying those of the enemy.

2. I know how, in the course of the siege of a terrain, to remove water from the moats and how to make an infinite number of bridges, mantlets and scaling ladders and other instruments necessary to such an enterprise.

3. Also, if one cannot, when besieging a terrain, proceed by bombardment either because of the height of the glacis or the strength of its situation and location, I have methods for destroying every fortress or other stranglehold unless it has been founded upon a rock or so forth.

4. I have also types of cannon, most convenient and easily portable, with which to hurl small stones almost like a hail-storm; and the smoke from the cannon will instil a great fear in the enemy on account of the grave damage and confusion.

5. Also, I have means of arriving at a designated spot through mines and secret winding passages constructed completely without noise, even if it should be necessary to pass underneath moats or any river.

6. Also, I will make covered vehicles, safe and unassailable, which will penetrate the enemy and their artillery, and there is no host of armed men so great that they would not break through it. And behind these the infantry will be able to follow, quite uninjured and unimpeded.

7. Also, should the need arise, I will make cannon, mortar and light ordnance of very beautiful and functional design that are quite out of the ordinary.

8. Where the use of cannon is impracticable, I will assemble catapults, mangonels, trebuckets and other instruments of wonderful efficiency not in general use. In short, as the variety of circumstances dictate, I will make an infinite number of items for attack and defence.

9. And should a sea battle be occasioned, I have examples of many instruments which are highly suitable either in attack or defence, and craft which will resist the fire of all the heaviest cannon and powder and smoke.

10. In time of peace I believe I can give as complete satisfaction as any other in the field of architecture, and the construction of both public and private buildings, and in conducting water from one place to another.

Also I can execute sculpture in marble, bronze and clay. Likewise in painting,[3] I can do everything possible as well as any other, whosoever he may be.

Moreover, work could be undertaken on the bronze horse which will be to the immortal glory and eternal honour of the auspicious memory of His Lordship your father, and of the illustrious house of Sforza.

And if any of the above-mentioned things seem impossible or impracticable to anyone, I am most readily disposed to demonstrate them in your park or in whatsoever place shall please Your Excellency, to whom I commend myself with all possible humility.

---

3 This letter achieved its purpose. Sforza hired Leonardo da Vinci, and in 1495, commissioned him to paint *The Last Supper.*

I Discovered a Great Many Islands

Christopher Columbus' letter to Luis de Santángel, dated 1493

As I know you will be rejoiced at the glorious success that our Lord has given me in my voyage, I write this to tell you how in thirty-three days I sailed to the Indies with the fleet that the illustrious King and Queen, our Sovereigns, gave me, where I discovered a great many islands,[1] inhabited by numberless people; and of all I have taken possession for their Highnesses by proclamation and display of the Royal Standard without opposition.[2] To the first island I discovered I gave the name of San Salvador, in commemoration of His Divine Majesty, who has wonderfully granted all this. The Indians call it Guanaham. The second I named the Island of

---

1 The location of the island where Columbus' ship, Santa Maria landed is not clear, but it was somewhere in the modern-day Bahamas.

2 Columbus, upon landing on the island, had presented red hats and beads to the natives, who, in turn, gifted him parrots, cotton, and other goods.

Santa Maria de Concepcion; the third, Fernandina; the fourth, Isabella; the fifth, Juana; and thus to each one I gave a new name. When I came to Juana, I followed the coast of that isle toward the west, and found it so extensive that I thought it might be the mainland, the province of Cathay; and as I found no towns nor villages on the sea-coast, except a few small settlements, where it was impossible to speak to the people, because they fled at once, I continued the said route, thinking I could not fail to see some great cities or towns; and finding at the end of many leagues that nothing new appeared, and that the coast led northward, contrary to my wish, because the winter had already set in, I decided to make for the south, and as the wind also was against my proceeding, I determined not to wait there longer, and turned back to a certain harbor whence I sent two men to find out whether there was any king or large city. They explored for three days, and found countless small communities and people, without number, but with no kind of government, so they returned.

I heard from other Indians I had already taken that this land was an island, and thus followed the eastern coast for one hundred and seven leagues, until I came to the end of it. From that point I saw another isle to the eastward, at eighteen leagues' distance, to which I gave the name of Hispaniola. I went thither and followed its northern coast to the east, as I had done in Juana, one hundred and seventy-eight leagues eastward, as in Juana. This island, like all the others, is most extensive. It has many ports along the sea-coast excelling any in Christendom — and many fine, large, flowing rivers. The land there is elevated, with many mountains and peaks incomparably higher than in the centre isle. They are most beautiful, of a thousand varied forms, accessible, and full of trees of endless varieties, so high that they seem to touch the sky, and I have been told that they never lose their foliage. I saw them as green and lovely as trees are in Spain in the month of May. Some of them were covered with blossoms, some with fruit, and some in other conditions, according to their kind. The nightingale and other small birds of a thousand kinds were singing in the month of November when I was there. There were palm trees of six or eight varieties, the graceful peculiarities of each one of them being worthy of admiration as are the other trees, fruits and grasses. There are wonderful pine woods, and very extensive ranges of meadow land. There is honey, and there are many kinds of birds, and a great variety of fruits. Inland there are numerous mines of metals and innumerable people. Hispaniola is a marvel. Its hills and mountains, fine plains and open country, are rich and fertile for planting and for pasturage, and for building towns and villages. The seaports there are incredibly fine, as also the magnificent rivers, most of which bear gold. The trees, fruits and grasses differ widely from those in Juana. There are many spices and vast mines of gold and other metals in this island. They have no iron, nor steel, nor weapons, nor are they fit for them, because although they are well-made men of commanding stature, they appear extraordinarily timid. The only arms they have are sticks of cane, cut when in seed, with a sharpened stick at the end, and they are afraid to use these. Often I have sent two or three men ashore to some town to converse with them, and the natives came out in great numbers, and as soon as they saw our men arrive, fled without a moment's delay although I protected them from all injury.

At every point where I landed, and succeeded in talking to them, I gave them some of everything I had — cloth and many other things — without receiving anything in return, but they are a hopelessly timid people. It is true that since they have gained more confidence and are losing this fear, they are so unsuspicious and so generous with what they possess, that no one who had not seen it would believe it. They never refuse anything that is asked for. They even offer it themselves, and show so much love that they would give their very hearts. Whether it be anything of great or small value, with any trifle of whatever kind, they are satisfied. I forbade worthless things being given to them, such as bits of broken bowls, pieces of glass, and old straps, although they were as much pleased to get them as if they were the finest jewels in the world. One sailor was found to have got for a leathern strap, gold of the weight of two and a half castellanos, and others for even more worthless things much more; while for a new blancas they would give all they had, were it two or three castellanos of pure gold or an arroba or two of spun cotton. Even bits of the broken hoops of wine casks they accepted, and gave in return what they had, like fools, and it seemed wrong to me. I forbade it, and gave a thousand good and pretty things that I had to win their love, and to induce them to become Christians, and to love and serve their Highnesses and the whole Castilian nation, and help to get for us things they have in abundance, which are necessary to us. They have no religion, nor idolatry, except that they all believe power and goodness to be in heaven. They firmly believed that I, with my ships and men, came from heaven, and with this idea I have been received everywhere, since they lost fear of me. They are, however, far from being ignorant. They are most ingenious men, and navigate these seas in a wonderful way, and describe everything well, but they never before saw people wearing clothes, nor vessels like ours. Directly I reached the Indies in the first isle I discovered, I took by force some of the natives, that from them we might gain some information of what there was in these parts; and so it was that we immediately understood each other, either by words or signs. They are still with me and still believe that I come from heaven. They were the first to declare this wherever I went, and the others ran from house to house, and to the towns around, crying out, "Come! come! and see the man from heaven!" Then all, both men and women, as soon as they were reassured about us, came, both small and great, all bringing something to eat and to drink, which they presented with marvellous kindness. In these isles there are a great many canoes, something like rowing boats, of all sizes, and most of them are larger than an eighteen-oared galley. They are not so broad, as they are made of a single plank, but a galley could not keep up with them in rowing, because they go with incredible speed, and with these they row about among all these islands, which are innumerable, and carry on their commerce. I have seen some of these canoes with seventy and eighty men in them, and each had an oar. In all the islands I observed little difference in the appearance of the people, or in their habits and language, except that they understand each other, which is remarkable. Therefore I hope that their Highnesses will decide upon the conversion of these people to our holy faith, to which they seem much inclined.[3] I have already stated how I sailed one hundred and seven leagues along the sea-coast of Juana, in a straight line from west to east. I can therefore assert that this island is larger than England and Scotland together, since beyond these one hundred and seven leagues there remained at the west

---

3 Columbus knew that merely invading the Americas would not be sufficient to completely possess the islands. Following the discovery, he immediately put forward his motive to evangelize the natives in order to strengthen their control over the invaded territory.

point two provinces where I did not go, one of which they call Avan, the home of men with tails. These provinces are computed to be fifty or sixty leagues in length, as far as can be gathered from the Indians with me, who are acquainted with all these islands. This other, Hispaniola, is larger in circumference than all Spain from Catalonia to Fuentarabia in Biscay, since upon one of its four sides I sailed one hundred and eighty-eight leagues from west to east. This is worth having, and must on no account be given up. I have taken possession of all these islands, for their Highnesses, and all may be more extensive than I know, or can say, and I hold them for their Highnesses, who can command them as absolutely as the kingdoms of Castile. In Hispaniola, in the most convenient place, most accessible for the gold mines and all commerce with the mainland on this side or with that of the great Khan, on the other, with which there would be great trade and profit, I have taken possession of a large town, which I have named the City of Navidad. I began fortifications there which should be completed by this time, and I have left in it men enough to hold it, with arms, artillery, and provisions for more than a year; and a boat with a master seaman skilled in the arts necessary to make others; I am so friendly with the king of that country that he was proud to call me his brother and hold me as such. Even should he change his mind and wish to quarrel with my men, neither he nor his subjects know what arms are, nor wear clothes, as I have said. They are the most timid people in the world, so that only the men remaining there could destroy the whole region, and run no risk if they know how to behave themselves properly. In all these islands the men seem to be satisfied with one wife except they allow as many as twenty to their chief or men. The women appear to me to work harder than the men, and so far as I can hear they have nothing of their own, for I think I perceived that what one had others shared, especially food. In the islands so far, I have found no monsters, as some expected, but, on the contrary, they are people of very handsome appearance. They are not black as in Guinea, though their hair is straight and coarse, as it does not grow where the sun's rays are too ardent. And in truth the sun has extreme power here, since it is within twenty-six degrees of the equinoctial line. In these islands there are mountains where the cold this winter was very severe, but the people endure it from habit, and with the aid of the meat they eat with very hot spices.

As for monsters, I have found not trace of them except at the point in the second isle as one enters the Indies, which is inhabited by a people considered in all the isles as most ferocious, who eat human flesh. They possess many canoes, with which they overrun all the isles of India, stealing and seizing all they can. They are not worse looking than the others, except that they wear their hair long like women, and use bows and arrows of the same cane, with a sharp stick at the end for want of iron, of which they have none. They are ferocious compared to these other races, who are extremely cowardly; but I only hear this from the others. They are said to make treaties of marriage with the women in the first isle to be met with coming from Spain to the Indies, where there are no men. These women have no feminine occupation, but use bows and arrows of cane like those before mentioned, and cover and arm themselves with plates of copper, of which they have a great quantity. Another island, I am told, is larger than Hispaniola, where the natives have no hair, and where there is countless gold; and from them all I bring Indians to testify to this. To speak, in conclusion, only of what has been done during this hurried voyage, their Highnesses will see that I can give them as much gold as they desire, if they will give me a little assistance, spices, cotton, as much as their Highnesses may command to be shipped, and mastic as much as their Highnesses choose to send for, which until now has only been found in Greece, in the isle of Chios, and the Signoria can get its own price for it; as much lign-aloe as they command to be shipped, and as many slaves as they choose to send for, all heathens. I think I have found rhubarb and cinnamon. Many other things of value will be discovered by the men I left behind me, as I stayed nowhere when the wind allowed me to pursue my voyage, except in the City of Navidad, which I left fortified and safe. Indeed, I might have accomplished much more, had the crews served me as they ought to have done. The eternal and almighty God, our Lord, it is Who gives to all who walk in His way, victory over things apparently impossible, and in this case signally so, because although these lands had been imagined and talked of before they were seen, most men listened incredulously to what was thought to be but an idle tale. But our Redeemer has given victory to our most illustrious King and Queen, and to their kingdoms rendered famous by this glorious event, at which all Christendom should rejoice, celebrating it with great festivities and solemn Thanksgivings to the Holy Trinity, with fervent prayers for the high distinction that will accrue to them from turning so many peoples to our holy faith; and also from the temporal benefits that not only Spain but all Christian nations will obtain. Thus I record what has happened in a brief note written on board the *Caravel*, off the Canary Isles, on the 15th of February, 1493.

Yours to command,
THE ADMIRAL

Postscript within the letter
Since writing the above, being in the Sea of Castile, so much wind arose south southeast, that I was forced to lighten the vessels, to run into this port of Lisbon today which was the most extraordinary thing in the world, from whence I resolved to write to their Highnesses. In all the Indies I always found the temperature like that

of May. Where I went in thirty-three days I returned in twenty-eight, except that these gales have detained me fourteen days, knocking about in this sea, Here all seamen say that there has never been so rough a winter, nor so many vessels lost. Done the 14th day of March.

The Sickness of My Mistress

King Henry VIII's letter to Anne Boleyn

June 1528

There came to me suddenly in the night the most afflicting news that could have arrived. The first, to hear of the sickness of my mistress,[1] whom I esteem more than all the world, and whose health I desire as I do my own, so that I would gladly bear half your illness to make you well. The second, from the fear that I have of being still longer harassed by my enemy. Absence, much longer, who has hitherto given me all possible uneasiness, and as far as I can judge is determined to spite me more because I pray God to rid me of this troublesome tormentor. The third, because the physician in whom I have most confidence, is absent at the very time when

---

1 Anne Boleyn married King Henry VIII in 1533, and became the Queen of England. However, their love story came to a horrific end. Three years later, she was charged with adultery and incest, and consequently, beheaded for conspiring against the King.

he might do me the greatest pleasure; for I should hope, by him and his means, to obtain one of my chief joys on earth — that is the care of my mistress — yet for want of him I send you my second, and hope that he will soon make you well. I shall then love him more than ever. I beseech you to be guided by his advice in your illness. In so doing I hope soon to see you again, which will be to me a greater comfort than all the precious jewels in the world.

Written by that secretary, who is, and for ever will be, your loyal and most assui'ed Servant,

H. (A B) R.

You Have Not a More Affectionate Relative in the World

Mary Stuart's letter to Queen Elizabeth, dated c. 1567-1568

Madame, my Good Sister

The length of my weary imprisonment,[1] and the wrongs I have received from those on whom I have conferred so many benefits, are less annoying to me than not having it in my power to acquaint you with the realities of my calamities, and the injuries that have been done to me in various ways. It may please you to remember that you have told me several times "that on receiving that ring you gave me, you would assist me in any time of trouble". You know that Lord James[2] has seized all I have. Melville, to whom I

---

1 Many Confederate Lords had started opposing Mary Stuart's rule ever since she had married Earl of Bothwell, the man rumoured to have murdered Mary's previous husband, Lord Darnley. Mary surrendered at the battle at Carberry Hill, and was imprisoned at Lochleven Castle in June 1567.

2 Mary had been devastated in prison. During her time there, she had been forced to abdicate her throne in favour of her son, James, and had miscarried a baby.

have often sent secretly for this ring, as my most precious jewel, says that he dare not let me have it. Therefore I implore you to have compassion on your good sister and cousin, and believe that you have not a more affectionate relative in the world.[3] You should also consider the importance of the example practised against me.

I entreat you to be careful that no one knows that I have written to you, for it would cause me to be treated worse than I am now. They boast that their friends at your court inform them of all you say and do. God keep you from misfortunes, and grant me patience and His grace that I may one day recount my calumnies to yourself, when I will tell you more than I dare to write, which may prove of no small service to yourself.

Your obliged and affectionate good sister and cousin,

(Signed Mary)

---

3 Queen Elizabeth considered Mary Stuart her enemy. Elizabeth's mother was Anne Boleyn, Henry VIII's second wife. Only two years after Elizabeth was born, their marriage was annulled, and thus, Elizabeth became illegitimate for the throne in the eyes of many people. Contrastingly, Mary Stuart was a descendant of Henry VIII's elder sister, thereby giving her a rightful claim to the English throne. Elizabeth felt threatened by her, which is why Mary assures her here that now, she only wishes her well.

I Am to Be executed Like a Criminal

Mary Stuart's letter to Henry III
To Henri III[1], the Most Christian King of France

8 February 1587.

Royal brother, having by God's will, for my sins I think, thrown myself into the power of the Queen my cousin, at whose hands I have suffered much for almost twenty years, I have finally been condemned to death by her and her Estates. I have asked for my papers, which they have taken away, in order that I might make my will, but I have been unable to recover anything of use to me, or even get leave either to make my will freely or to have my body conveyed after my death, as I would wish, to your kingdom where I had honour to be queen, your sister and old ally.

Tonight, after dinner, I have been advised of my sentence: I am to be executed like a criminal at

1 Henry III was brother to Mary Stuart's first husband.

eight in the morning.[2] I have not had time to give you a full account of everything that has happened, but if you will listen to my doctor and my other unfortunate servants, you will learn the truth, and how, thanks be to God, I scorn death and vow that I meet it innocent of any crime,[3] even if I were their subject. The Catholic faith and the assertion of my God-given right to the English throne are the two issues on which I am condemned, and yet I am not allowed to say that it is for the Catholic religion that I die, but for fear of interference with theirs. The proof of this is that they have taken away my chaplain, and, although he is in the building, I have not been able to get permission for him to come and hear my confession and give me the Last Sacrament, while they have been most insistent that I receive the consolation and instruction of their minister brought here for that purpose.

The bearer of this letter and his companions, most of them your subjects, will testify to my conduct at my last hour. It remains for me to beg Your Most Christian Majesty, my brother-in-law and old ally, who have always

---

2 On 8 February 1857, six hours after writing this letter, Mary Stuart was beheaded on the orders of her cousin, Queen Elizabeth I.

3 After being imprisoned at the Lochleven Castle for a year, Mary Stuart managed to escape to England and requested her cousin to give her refuge. Instead of giving her support, Elizabeth gave orders to capture her, and twenty years later, ordered her execution.

protested your love for me, to give proof now of your goodness on all these points: firstly by charity, in paying my unfortunate servants the wages due to them-this is a burden on my conscience that only you can relieve: further, by having prayers offered to God for a queen who has borne the title Most Christian, and who dies a Catholic, stripped of all her possessions. As for my son, I commend him to you in so far as he deserves, for I cannot answer for him.

I have taken the liberty of sending you two precious stones, talismans against illness, trusting you will enjoy good health and a long and happy life. Accept them from your loving sister-in-law, who, as she dies, bears witness of her warm feelings for you. Again I commend my servants to you. Give instruction, if it please you, that for my soul's sake part of what you owe me should be paid, and that for the sake of Jesus Christ, to whom I shall pray for you tomorrow as I die, I be left enough to found a memorial mass and give the customary alms.

Wednesday at two in the morning.

Your most loving and most true sister.

(Signed Mary)

You Are Now My Enemy

Benjamin Franklin's letter to William Strahan

5 July 1775[1]

Mr. Strahan

You are a Member of Parliament, and one of that Majority which has doomed my Country to Destruction. You have begun to burn our Towns and murder our People. — Look upon your hands! They are stained with the Blood of your Relations! — You and I were long Friends:[2]— You are now my Enemy,[3] — and

I am,

Yours.

B. Franklin

---

1 The year when the American Revolutionary War started.

2 William Strahan had been a friend to Benjamin Franklin for thirty years till then.

3 Franklin was in a rage because according to him, Strahan had changed his stance on the American Revolutionary War after becoming a printer to the King, advocating that force should be used to bring the masses down. However, Franklin wisely decided not to send the letter, and resumed his friendship following the War's conclusion.

I Detest You

Napoleon Bonaparte's letter to Josephine

Verona, November 23, 1796.

I don't love you an atom; on the contrary, I detest you. You are a good for nothing, very ungraceful, very tactless, very tatterdemalion. You never write to me; you don't care for your husband; you know the pleasure your letters give him, and you write him barely half-a-dozen lines, thrown off anyhow.

How, then, do you spend the livelong day, madam? What business of such importance robs you of the time to write to your very kind lover? What inclination stifles and alienates love, the affectionate and unvarying love which you promised me? Who may this paragon be, this new lover who engrosses all your time, is master of your days, and prevents you from concerning yourself about your husband?[1] Josephine, be

---

1 Napoleon's suspicion of Josephine of having an extra-marital affair turned out to be true. While he was busy amassing victories in Italy, Josephine was eyeing Hussar regiment's lieutenant, Charles Hippolyte, a man almost a decade younger to her.

vigilant; one fine night the doors will be broken in, and I shall be before you.

Truly, my dear, I am uneasy at getting no news from you. Write me four pages immediately, and some of those charming remarks which fill my heart with the pleasures of imagination.

I hope that before long I shall clasp you in my arms, and cover you with a million kisses as burning as if under the equator.

BONAPARTE.

Remain My True and Only Treasure

Ludwig van Beethoven's letter to his Immortal Beloved, written in 1812

6 July, morning

My angel, my all, my own self — only a few words today, and that too with pencil (with yours) — only till tomorrow is my lodging definitely fixed. What abominable waste of time in such things — why this deep grief, where necessity speaks?

Can our love persist otherwise than through sacrifices, than by not demanding everything? Canst thou change it, that thou are not entirely mine, I not entirely thine? Oh, God, look into beautiful Nature and compose your mind to the inevitable. Love demands everything and is quite right, so it is for me with you,[1] for you with me — only you forget so easily, that I must live

1 The identity of Beethoven's beloved is still unknown. Some people believe her to be Antonie Brentano, others believe her to be Josephine von Brunswik, but no one has been able to establish her identity without a doubt.

for you and for me — were we quite united, you would notice this painful feeling as little as I should . . .

. . . We shall probably soon meet, even today I cannot communicate my remarks to you, which during these days I made about my life — were our hearts close together, I should probably not make any such remarks. My bosom is full, to tell you much — there are moments when I find that speech is nothing at all. Brighten up — remain my true and only treasure, my all, as I to you. The rest the gods must send, what must be for us and shall.

Your faithful

Ludwig

Is This the Way That We Are to Live

Mary Shelley's letter to P B Shelley, dated 1814

For what a minute did I see you yesterday – is this the way my beloved that we are to live[1] till the sixth in the morning I look for you and when I awake I turn to look on you – dearest Shelley you are solitary and uncomfortable why cannot I be with you to cheer you and to press you to my heart oh my love you have no friends why then should you be torn from the only one who has affection for you – But I shall see you tonight and that is the hope that I shall live on through the day– be happy dear Shelley and think of me – why do I say this dearest & only one I know how tenderly you love me and how you repine at this absence from me – when shall we be free from fear of treachery?

---

1 P B Shelley's financial situation was incredibly precarious by now. The creditors were literally at his door, demanding what they were owed. He had been hiding to escape them, trying to arrange funds. Somehow, Shelley managed to meet Mary for a brief time at a coffee house, the day before.

I send you the letter I told you of from Harriet[2] and a letter we received yesterday from fanny the history of this interview I will tell you when I come – but perhaps as it is so rainy a day Fanny will not be allowed to come at all –

My love my own one be happy –

I was so dreadfully tired yesterday that I was obliged to take a coach home forgive this extravagance but I am so very weak at present & I had been so agitated through the day that I was not able to stand a morning rest however will set me quite right again and I shall be quite well when I meet you this evening – will you be at the door of the coffee house at five oclock as it is désagreable to go into those places and I shall be there exactly at the time & we will go into St. Pauls where we can sit down.

I send you Diogenes as you have no books – Hookham was so ill tempered as not to send the books I asked for.

---

2 Harriet Westbrook was P B Shelley's first wife. When they had eloped in 1811, Harriet was only sixteen, and P B Shelley was nineteen years old. Three years later, around the time Harriet got pregnant, P B Shelley eloped with Mary Godwin. In 1816, Harriet committed suicide.

I Could
Die for You

John Keats' letter[1] to Fanny Brawne

October 13, 1819

My dearest Girl,

This moment I have set myself to copy some verses out fair. I cannot proceed with any degree of content. I must write you a line or two and see if that will assist in dismissing you from my Mind for ever so short a time. Upon my Soul I can think of nothing else – The time is passed when I had power to advise and warn you against the unpromising morning of my Life – My love[2] has made me selfish. I cannot exist without you – I am forgetful of every thing but

---

1 All the love letters from John Keats to Fanny Brawne were published in 1878.

2 The love story of John Keats and Fanny Brawne started in 1819. But their romance was kept a secret. Brawne was married. Keats would have been unable to support a wife since he had chosen to pursue poetry as a career, that too at a time when his family was ankle-deep in a financial crisis.

seeing you again – my Life seems to stop there – I see no further. You have absorb'd me. I have a sensation at the present moment as though I was dissolving – I should be exquisitely miserable without the hope of soon seeing you. I should be afraid to separate myself far from you. My sweet Fanny, will your heart never change? My love, will it? I have no limit now to my love – You note came in just here – I cannot be happier away from you – 'T is richer than an Argosy of Pearles. Do not threat me even in jest. I have been astonished that Men could die Martyrs for religion – I have shudder'd at it – I shudder no more – I could be martyr'd for my Religion – Love is my religion – I could die for that – I could die for you. My Creed is Love and you are its only tenet – You have ravish'd me away by a Power I cannot resist: and yet I could resist till I saw you; and even since I have seen you I have endeavoured often "to reason against the reasons of my Love." I can do that no more – the pain would be too great – My Love is selfish – I cannot breathe without you.

Yours for ever
John Keats

I Have Done All in My Power

Charles Dickens' letter to Edgar Allan Poe

London, 1 Devonshire Terrace,
York Gate, Regent's Park,
November 27, 1842.

Dear Sir, — by some strange accident (I presume it must have been through some mistake on the part of Mr. Putnam in the great quantity of business he had to arrange for me), I have never been able to find among my papers, since I came to England, the letter you wrote to me at New York. But I read it there, and think I am correct in believing that it charged me with no other mission than that which you had already entrusted to me by word of mouth. Believe me that it never, for a moment, escaped my recollection; and that I have done all in my power to bring it to a successful issue — I regret to say, in vain.[1]

---

1 Charles Dickens was in Philadelphia to give a lecture that year, and Edgar Allan Poe had requested a meeting. Dickens had agreed to meet him the next day. Among discussing other things, Dickens had promised to help Poe in finding someone to publish Poe's work in New York but he had been unsuccessful.

I should have forwarded you the accompanying letter from Mr. Moxon before now, but that I have delayed doing so in the hope that some other channel for the publication of our book on this side of the water would present itself to me. I am, however, unable to report any success. I have mentioned it to publishers with whom I have influence, but they have, one and all, declined the venture. And the only consolation I can give you is that I do not believe any collection of detached pieces by an unknown writer, even though he were an Englishman, would be at all likely to find a publisher in this metropolis just now.

Do not for a moment suppose that I have ever thought of you but with a pleasant recollection; and that I am not at all times prepared to forward your views in this country, if I can.

Faithfully yours,
Charles Dickens.

Species Are Not Immutable

Charles Darwin's letter to Joseph D Hooker, dated 1844

Down. Bromley Kent

Thursday

My dear Sir

I must write to thank you for your last letter; I to tell you how much all your views and facts interest me. — I must be allowed to put my own interpretation on what you say of "not being a good arranger of extended views" — which is, that you do not indulge in the loose speculations so easily started by every smatterer & wandering collector. — I look at a strong tendency to generalize as an entire evil —

What limit shall you take on the Patagonian side — has d'Orbigny published, I believe he made a large collection at the R. Negro, where Patagonia retains its usual forlorn appearance; at Bahia

Blanca & northward the features of Patagonia insensibly blend into the savannahs of La Plata. — The Botany of S. Patagonia (& I collected every plant in flower at the season when there) would be worth comparison with the N. Patagonian collection by d'Orbigny. — I do not know anything about King's plants, but his birds were so inaccurately habitated, that I have seen specimen from Brazil, Tierra del & the Cape de Verde Isd all said to come from the St. Magellan. — What you say of Mr Brown is humiliating; I had suspected it, but cd not allow myself to believe in such heresy. — FitzRoy gave him a rap in his Preface, & made me very indignant, but it seems a much harder one wd not have been wasted. My crptogamic collection was sent to Berkeley; it was not large; I do not believe he has yet published an account, but he wrote to me some year ago that he had described & mislaid all his descriptions. Wd it not be well for you to put yourself in communication with him; as otherwise some things will perhaps be twice laboured over. — My best (though poor) collection of the Crptogam. was from the Chonos Islands. —

Would you kindly observe one little fact for me, whether any species of plant, peculiar to any isld, as Galapagos, St. Helena or New Zealand, where there are no large quadrupeds, have hooked seeds, — such hooks as if observed here would be thought with justness to be adapted to catch into wool of animals. —

Would you further oblige me some time by informing me (though I forget this will certainly appear in your Antarctic Flora) whether in isld like St. Helena, Galapagos, & New Zealand, the number of families & genera are large compared with the number of species, as happens in coral-isld, & as I believe? in the extreme Arctic land. Certainly this is case with Marine shells in extreme Arctic seas. — Do you suppose the fewness of species in proportion to number of large groups in Coral-islets., is owing to the chance of seeds from all orders, getting drifted to such new spots? as I have supposed. —

Did you collect sea-shells in Kerguelen land, I shd like to know their character.?

Your interesting letters tempt me to be very unreasonable in asking you questions; but you must not give yourself any trouble about them, for I know how fully & worthily you are employed.

Besides a general interest about the Southern lands, I have been now ever since my return engaged in a very presumptuous work & which I know no one individual who wd not say a very foolish one. — I was so struck with distribution of Galapagos organisms &c &c & with the character of the American fossil mammifers, &c &c that I determined to collect blindly every sort of fact, which cd bear any way on what are species. — I have read heaps of agricultural & horticultural books, & have never ceased collecting facts — At last gleams of light have come, & I am almost convinced (quite contrary to opinion I started with) that species are not (it is like confessing a murder) immutable.[1] Heaven forfend me from Lamarck nonsense of a "tendency to progression" "adaptations from the slow willing of animals"[2] &c, — but the conclusions I am led to are not widely different from his — though the means of change are wholly so — I think I have found out (here's presumption!) the simple way by which species become exquisitely adapted to various ends. — You will now groan, & think to yourself 'on what a man have I been wasting my time in writing to.'[3] — I shd, five years ago, have thought so. — I fear you will also groan at the length

---

1 This was the first time Darwin had mentioned his theory of evolution to someone else.

2 Darwin's theory was that all organisms evolve to adapt to and survive in their changing environment through a process of natural selection of the mutations in their bodies. *The Origin of Species* came out with this, fifteen years after Darwin wrote this letter, proving that man has descended from apes.

3 The reception of Darwin's evolution theory evinced a mixed response at the time of its publication. Naturally, the religious sects were outraged since this contradicted with their espousing of the belief that man was shaped in God's image. Joseph Hooker, however, supported Darwin when Darwin's theory was discussed at the Oxford University Museum in 1860, seven months after *The Origin of Species* was published.

of this letter — excuse me, I did not begin with malice prepense.

Believe me my dear Sir
Very truly your's
C. Darwin

I Love Now for the First and Only Time

Edgar Allan Poe's letter to Sarah Helen Whitman

Sunday Night — Oct. 1 — 48.

In pressing my last letter between your dear hands, there passed into your spirit a sense of the *Love* that glowed within those pages: — you say this, and I feel that indeed it *must* have been so: — but. in receiving the paper upon which your eyes now rest, did no shadow steal over you, from the *Sorrow* within, — oh God! how I now curse the impotence of the pen — the inexorable distance between us! I am pining to speak to *you*, Helen, — to you in person — to be near you while I speak — gently to press your hand in mine — to look into your soul through your eyes — and thus to *be sure* that my voice passes into your heart. Only thus could I hope to make you understand what I feel; and even thus I *should* not hope to make you do so; for it is only Love, which can comprehend Love — and alas! you do not love me. — Bear with me! have patience with me! — for indeed my heart is broken; and, let me struggle as I will, I cannot *write* to you the calm, cold language of a world which I loathe — of a world in which I have no interest — of a world which is not mine. I repeat to you that my heart is broken — that I have no farther object in life — that I have absolutely no wish but *to die*. These are hackneyed phrases; but they will not now impress you as such — for you must and do know the passionate agony with which I write them. "You do not love me": — in this brief sentence lies all I can conceive of despair. I have no resource — no hope: — Pride itself fails me now. You do not love me; or you could not have imposed upon me the torture of eight days' silence — of eight days' terrible suspense. You do not love me — or, responding to my prayers, you would have cried to me — "Edgar, I do." Ah, Helen, the emotion which now consumes me teaches me too well the nature of the impulses of Love! Of what avail to me, in my deadly grief, are your enthusiastic words of mere admiration? Alas! — alas! — I have been loved, and a relentless Memory contrasts what you say with the unheeded, unvalued language of others. — But ah, — again, and most especially — you do not love me, or you would have felt too thorough a sympathy with the sensitiveness of my nature, to have so wounded me as you have done with this terrible passage of your letter: —"How often I have heard men and even women say of you —'He has great intellectual power, but no principle — no moral sense.'" Is it possible that such expressions as these could have been repeated to me — to me — by one whom I loved — ah, whom I love — by one at whose feet I knelt — I still kneel — in deeper worship than ever man offered to God? — And you proceed to ask me why such opinions exist. You will feel remorse for the question, Helen, when I say to you that, until the moment when those horrible words first met my eye, I would not have believed it *possible* that any such opinions could have existed at all: — but that they do exist breaks my heart in separating us forever. I love you too truly ever to have offered you my hand — ever to have sought your love — had I *known* my name to be so stained as your expressions imply. — Oh God! what shall *I* say to you Helen, dear Helen? — let me call you now by that sweet name, if I may never so call you again. — It is altogether in vain that I tax my Memory or my Conscience. There is no oath which seems to me so sacred as that sworn by the all-divine love I bear you. — By this love, then, and by the God who reigns in Heaven, I swear to you that my soul is incapable of dishonor — that, with the exception of occasional follies and excesses which I bitterly lament, but to which I have been driven by intolerable sorrow, and which are hourly committed by others without attracting any notice whatever — I can call to mind no act of my life which would bring a blush to my cheek — or to yours. If I have erred at all, in this regard, it has been on the side of what the world would call a Quixotic sense of the honorable — of the chivalrous. The indulgence of this sense has been the true voluptuousness of my life. It was for this species of luxury that, in early youth, I deliberately threw away from me a large fortune, rather than endure a trivial wrong. It was for this that, at a later period, I did violence to my own heart, and married, for another's happiness, where I knew that no possibility of my own existed. — Ah, how profound is my love for you, since it forces me into these egotisms for which you will inevitably despise me! Nevertheless, I must now speak to you the truth or nothing. It was in mere indulgence, then, of the sense to which I refer, that, at one dark epoch of my late life, for the sake of one who, deceiving and betraying, still loved me much, I sacrificed what seemed in the eyes of men my honor, rather than abandon what was honor in hers and in my own. — But, alas! for nearly three years I have been ill, poor, living out of the world; and thus, as I now painfully see, have afforded opportunity to my enemies — and especially to one, the most malignant and pertinacious of all fiends next line was obliterated and then continues] to slander me, in private society, without my knowledge and thus with impunity. Although much, however, may (and I now see must) have been said to my discredit, during my retirement, those few who, knowing me well, have been steadfastly my friends, permitted nothing to reach my ears — unless in one instance, where the malignity of the accuser hurried her beyond her usual caution, and thus the accusation was of such character that I could appeal to a court of justice for redress. The tools employed in this instance were Mr. Hiram Fuller and Mr. T. D. English. I replied to the charge fully, in a public newspaper — afterwards suing the "Mirror" (in which the scandal appeared) obtaining a verdict and recovering such an amount of damages as, for the time, completely to break up that journal. — And you ask me *why* men so misjudge me — why I have enemies. If your knowledge of my character and of my career does not afford you an answer to the query, at least it does not become me to suggest the answer. Let it suffice that I have had the audacity to remain poor that I might preserve my independence — that, nevertheless, in letters, to a certain extent and in certain regards, I have been "successful" — that I have been a critic — and unscrupulously honest and no doubt in many cases a bitter one — that I have uniformly attacked — where I attacked at all — those who stood highest in power and influence — and that, whether in literature or in society, I have seldom refrained from expressing, either directly or indirectly, the pure contempt with which the pretensions of ignorance, arrogance, or imbecility inspire me. — And you who know all this — *you* ask me *why* I have enemies. Ah, Helen, I have a hundred friends for every individual enemy — but has it never occurred to you that you do not live among my friends? Miss Lynch, Miss Fuller, Miss Blackwell, Mrs. Ellet — neither these nor any within their influence, are my friends. Had you read my criticisms generally, you would see, too, how and why it is that the Channings — the Emerson and Hudson coterie — the Longfellow clique, one and all — the cabal of the "N. American Review" — you would see why all these, whom *you* know best, know me least and are my enemies. Do you not remember with how deep a sigh I said to you in Providence — "My heart is heavy, Helen, for I see that your friends are not my own." — But the cruel sentence in your letter would not — could not so deeply have wounded me, had my soul been first strengthened by those assurances of your love which I so wildly — so vainly — and, I now feel, so presumptuously entreated. That our souls are one, every line which you have ever written asserts — but our hearts do not beat in unison. Tell me, darling! to your heart has any angel ever whispered that the very noblest lines in all human poetry are these — hackneyed though they be?

I know not — I ask not if guilt's in thy heart: —

I but know that *I love thee* whatever thou art.

When I first read your letter I could do nothing but shed tears, while I repeated, again and again, those glorious, those all-comprehensive verses, till I could scarcely hear my own voice for the passionate throbbings of my heart.

Forgive me, best and only beloved Helen, if there be bitterness in my tone. Towards *you* there is no room in my soul for any other sentiment than devotion: — it is Fate only which I accuse: — it is my own unhappy nature which wins me the true *love* of no woman whom by any possibility I could love.

I heard something, a day or two ago, which, had your last letter never reached me, might not irreparably have disturbed the relations between us, but which, as it is, withers forever all the dear hopes upspringing in my bosom. — A few words will explain to you what I mean. Not long after the receipt of your Valentine I learned, for the first time, that you were free — unmarried. I will not pretend to express to you what is absolutely inexpressible — that wild — long-enduring thrill of joy which pervaded my whole being on hearing that it was not *impossible* I might one day call you by the sacred title, wife: — but there was one alloy to this happiness: — I *dreaded* to find you in worldly circumstances superior to my own. Let me speak freely to you *now,* Helen, for perhaps I may never thus be permitted to speak to you again — Let me speak openly — fearlessly — trusting to the generosity of your own spirit for a true interpretation of my own. I repeat, then, that I *dreaded* to find you in worldly circumstances superior to mine. So great was my *fear* that you were rich, or at least possessed some property which might cause you to seem rich in the eyes of one so poor as I had always permitted myself to be — that, on the day I refer to, I had not the courage to ask my informant any questions concerning you. — I feel that you will have difficulty in comprehending me; but the horror with which, during my sojourn in the world, I have seen affection made a subject of barter, had, long since, — long before my marriage — inspired me with the resolution that, under *no* circumstances, would I marry where "interest," as the world terms it, could be suspected as, on my part, the object of the marriage. As far as this point concerned yourself, however, I was relieved, the next day, by an assurance that you were wholly dependent upon your mother. May I — dare I add — can you believe me when I say that this assurance was rendered doubly grateful to me by the additional one that you were in ill health and had suffered more from domestic sorrow than falls usually to the lot of woman? — and even if your faith in my nature is not too greatly tasked by such an assertion, can you forbear thinking me unkind, selfish or ungenerous? You cannot: — but oh! the sweet dreams which absorbed me at once: — dear dreams of a devotional care for you that should end only with life — of a tender, cherishing, patient solicitude which should bring you back, at length, to health and to happiness — a care — a solicitude — which should find its glorious reward in winning me, after long years, that which I could *feel* to be *your love!* —without well understanding *why,* I had been led to fancy you ambitious: — perhaps the fancy arose from your lines:

Not a bird that roams the forest
Shall our lofty eyrie share! —

but my very soul glowed with ambition for *your* sake, although I have always contemned it for my own. It was then only — then when I thought of you — that I dwelt exultingly upon what I felt that I could accomplish in Letters and in Literary Influence — in the widest and noblest field of human ambition.

"I will erect", I said, "a prouder throne than any on which mere monarch ever sat; and on this throne she — *she* shall be my queen". When I saw you, however — when I touched your gentle hand — when I heard your soft voice, and perceived how greatly I had misinterpreted your womanly nature — these triumphant visions melted sweetly away in the sunshine of a love ineffable; and I suffered my imagination to stray with you, and with the few who love us both, to the banks of some quiet river, in some lovely valley of our land. Here, not *too* far secluded from the world, we exercised a taste controlled by no conventionalities, but the sworn slave of a Natural Art, in the building for ourselves a cottage which no human being could ever pass without an ejaculation of wonder at its strange, weird, and incomprehensible yet most simple beauty. Oh, the sweet and gorgeous, but not often rare flowers in which we half buried it! — the grandeur of the little-distant magnolias and tulip-trees which stood guarding it — the luxurious velvet of its lawn — the lustre of the rivulet that ran by the very door — the tasteful yet quiet comfort of the interior — the music — the books — the unostentatious pictures — and, above all, the love — the *love* that threw an unfading *glory* over the whole! — Ah Helen! my heart is, indeed, breaking and I must now put an end to these divine dreams. Alas! all is now a dream; for I have lately heard that of you which, (taken in connexion with your letter and with that of which your letter does not assure me) puts it forever out of my power to ask you — again to ask you — to become my wife. That many persons, in your presence, have declared me wanting in honor, appeals irresistibly to an instinct of my nature — an instinct which *I feel* to be honor, let the dishonorable say what they may, and forbids me, under such circumstances, to insult you with my love: — but that you are quite independent in your worldly position (as I have just heard) — in a word *that you are comparatively rich while I am poor,* opens between us *a gulf* — a gulf, alas! which the sorrow and the slander of the World have rendered forever impassable — by me.

I have not yet been able to procure all the criticisms &c. of which you spoke, but will forward them, by express, in a day or two. Meantime I enclose the lines by Miss Fuller; and "The Domain of Arnheim" which happens to be at hand, and which, moreover, expresses *much of my soul.* — It was about the 10th of Sep., I think, that your sweet

MS. verses reached me in Richmond. I lectured in Lowell on the 10th of July. Your first letter was received by me, at Fordham, on the evening of Saturday, Sep. 30. I was in Providence, or its neighborhood, during the Monday you mention. In the morning I re-visited the cemetery: — at 6 P.M. I left the city in the Stonington train for N. Y. I cannot explain to you — since I cannot myself comprehend — the feeling which urged me not to see you again before going — not to bid you a second time *farewell.* I had a sad foreboding at heart. In the seclusion of the cemetery you sat by my side — on the very spot where my arm first tremblingly encircled your waist.

Edgar

My Heart Is Full of You

Emily Dickinson's letter to Susan Gilbert, dated 11 June 1852

Friday afternoon

I have but one thought, Susie,[1] this afternoon of June, and that of you, and I have one prayer, only; dear Susie, that is for you. That you and I in hand as we e'en *do* in heart, might ramble away as children, among the woods and fields, and forget these many years, and these sorrowing cares, and each become a child again — I would it were so, Susie, and when I look around me and find myself alone, I sigh for you again; little sigh, and vain sigh, which will not bring you home.

I need you more and more, and the great world grows wider, and dear ones fewer and fewer, every day that you stay away — I miss my biggest

---

1 Susan Gilbert and Emily Dickinson were close friends at the time. A year later, Susan married Austin Dickinson, Emily's brother.

heart; my own goes wandering round, and calls for Susie — Friends are too dear to sunder, Oh they are far too few, and how soon they will go away where you and I cannot find them, don't let us forget these things, for their remembrance now will save us many an anguish when it is too late to love them! Susie, forgive me Darling, for every word I say — my heart is full of you, none other than you is in my thoughts, yet when I seek to say to you something not for the world, words fail me.[2] If you were here — and Oh that you were, my Susie, we need not talk at all, our eyes would whisper for us, and your hand fast in mine, we would not ask for language — I try to bring you nearer, I chase the weeks away till they are quite departed, and fancy you have come, and I am on my way through the green lane to meet you, and my heart goes scampering so, that I have much ado to bring it back again, and learn it to be patient, till that dear Susie comes. Three weeks — they can't last always, for surely they must go with their little brothers and sisters to their long home in the west!

I shall grow more and more impatient until that dear day comes, for till now, I have only mourned for you; now I begin to hope for you.

---

2 The raw emotion and fierce, passionate evocation of Emily Dickinson's love for Susan Gilbert can be found in all of the letters of their correspondence. The exchange of letters started in 1850 and ended with Dickinson's death in 1886.

Dear Susie, I have tried hard to think what you would love, of something I might send you — I at last say my little Violets, they begged me to let <u>them</u> go, so here they are — and with them as Instructor, a bit of knightly grass, who also begged the favor to accompany them — they are but small, Susie, and I fear not fragrant now, but they will speak to you of warm hearts at home, and of something faithful which "never slumbers nor sleeps" — Keep them 'neath your pillow, Susie, they will make you dream of blue-skies, and home, and the "blessed contrie"! You and I will have an hour with "Edward" and "Ellen Middleton", sometime when you get home — we must find out if some things contained therein are true, and if they are, what you and me are coming to!

Now, farewell, Susie, and Vinnie sends her love, and mother her's, and I add a kiss, shyly, lest there is somebody there! Don't let them see, <u>will</u> you Susie? Emilie —

Why cant <u>I</u> be a Delegate to the great Whig Convention? - dont I know all about Daniel Webster, and the Tariff, and the Law? Then, Susie, I could see you, during a pause in the session - but I dont like this country at all, and I shant stay here any longer! "Delenda est" America, Massachusetts and all!

open me carefully -

You Would Be President

Grace Bedell's letter to Abraham Lincoln

Westfield Chatauque Co
Oct 15. 1860

Hon A B Lincoln
Dear Sir

My father has just home from the fair and brought home your picture and Mr. Hamlin's. I am a little girl only eleven years old, but want you should be President of the United States very much so I hope you wont think me very bold to write to such a great man as you are. Have you any little girls about as large as I am if so give them my love and tell her to write to me if you cannot answer this letter. I have got 4 brother's and part of them will vote for you any way and if you will let your whiskers grow I will try and get the rest of them to vote for you you would look a great deal better for your face is so thin. All the ladies like whiskers and they would tease their husband's to vote for you and then you would be President. My father is a going to vote for you and if I was a man I would vote for you[1] to but I will try and get every one to vote for you that I can I think that rail fence around your picture makes it look very pretty I have got a little baby sister she is nine weeks old and is just as cunning as can be. When you direct your letter direct to Grace Bedell Westfield Chatauque County New York

I must not write any more answer this letter right off
Good bye
Grace Bedell

---

1 Women gained their right to vote in 1919, with the passing of the nineteenth amendment in the Constitution.

What I Do About Slavery

Abraham Lincoln's letter to Horace Greeley[1]

Executive Mansion,

Washington, August 22, 1862.

Hon. Horace Greeley:

Dear Sir.

I have just read yours of the 19th. addressed to myself through the New-York Tribune. If there be in it any statements, or assumptions of fact, which I may know to be erroneous, I do not, now and here, controvert them. If there be in it any inferences which I may believe to be falsely drawn, I do not now and here, argue against them. If there be perceptable in it an impatient and dictatorial tone, I waive it in deference to

1 Horace Greeley was the editor of the New York *Tribune*, that he launched in 1841.

an old friend, whose heart I have always supposed to be right.

As to the policy I "seem to be pursuing" as you say, I have not meant to leave any one in doubt.

I would save the Union. I would save it the shortest way under the Constitution. The sooner the national authority can be restored; the nearer the Union will be "the Union as it was." If there be those who would not save the Union, unless they could at the same time save slavery, I do not agree with them. If there be those who would not save the Union unless they could at the same time destroy slavery, I do not agree with them. My paramount object in this struggle is to save the Union, and is not either to save or to destroy slavery. If I could save the Union without freeing any slave I would do it, and if I could save it by freeing all the slaves I would do it; and if I could save it by freeing some and leaving others alone I would also do that. What I do about slavery, and the colored race, I do because I believe it helps to save the Union;[2] and what I forbear, I forbear because I do not believe it would help to save the Union. I shall do less whenever I shall believe

---

2 Lincoln's response is to Greeley's demand in the article 'The Prayer of Twenty Millions' in *Tribune*, that the President abolish slavery for good. This happened a year after sending this letter. Abraham Lincoln brought about the Emancipation Proclamation, ordering the freedom of all slaves.

what I am doing hurts the cause, and I shall do more whenever I shall believe doing more will help the cause. I shall try to correct errors when shown to be errors; and I shall adopt new views so fast as they shall appear to be true views.

I have here stated my purpose according to my view of official duty; and I intend no modification of my oft-expressed personal wish that all men every where could be free.

Yours,
A. Lincoln

Do Whatever You Have to Do

Charles Dickens' letter to Edward Dickens, written c. 1868

My dearest Plorn,[1]

I write this note to-day because your going away is much upon my mind, and because I want you to have a few parting words from me to think of now and then at quiet times. I need not tell you that I love you dearly, and am very, very sorry in my heart to part with you. But this life is half made up of partings, and these pains must be borne. It is my comfort and my sincere conviction that you are going to try the life for which you are best fitted. I think its freedom and wildness more suited to you than any experiment in a study or office would ever have been; and without that training, you could have followed no other suitable occupation.

---

1 Plorn was the nickname of Charles Dickens' youngest son, Edward.

What you have already wanted until now has been a set, steady, constant purpose. I therefore exhort you to persevere in a thorough determination to do whatever you have to do as well as you can do it. I was not so old as you are now when I first had to win my food, and do this out of this determination, and I have never slackened in it since.

Never take a mean advantage of anyone in any transaction, and never be hard upon people who are in your power. Try to do to others, as you would have them do to you, and do not be discouraged if they fail sometimes. It is much better for you that they should fail in obeying the greatest rule laid down by our Saviour, than that you should.

I put a New Testament among your books, for the very same reasons, and with the very same hopes that made me write an easy account of it for you, when you were a little child; because it is the best book that ever was or will be known in the world, and because it teaches you the best lessons by which any human creature who tries to be truthful and faithful to duty can possibly be guided. As your brothers have gone away, one by one, I have written to each such words as I am now writing to you, and have entreated them all to guide themselves by this book, putting aside the interpretations and inventions of men.

You will remember that you have never at home been wearied about religious observances or mere formalities. I have always been anxious not to weary my children with such things before they are old enough to form opinions respecting them. You will therefore understand the better that I now most solemnly impress upon you the truth and beauty of the Christian religion, as it came from Christ Himself, and the impossibility of your going far wrong if you humbly but heartily respect it.

Only one thing more on this head. The more we are in earnest as to feeling it, the less we are disposed to hold forth about it. Never abandon the wholesome practice of saying your own private prayers, night and morning. I have never abandoned it myself, and I know the comfort of it.

I hope you will always be able to say in after life, that you had a kind father. You cannot show your affection for him so well, or make him so happy, as by doing your duty.

Your affectionate Father.

With You
One Must Be Open

Bram Stoker's letter to Walt Whitman

Dublin, Feb. 14, 1876.

My dear Mr. Whitman.

I hope you will not consider this letter from an utter stranger a liberty. Indeed, I hardly feel a stranger to you, nor is this the first letter that I have written to you. My friend Edward Dowden has told me often that you like new acquaintances or I should rather say friends. And as an old friend I send you an enclosure which may interest you. Four years ago I wrote the enclosed draft of a letter which I intended to copy out and send to you—it has lain in my desk since then—when I heard that you were addressed as Mr. Whitman. It speaks for itself and needs no comment. It is as truly what I wanted to say as that light is light.

The four years which have elapsed have made me love your work fourfold, and I can truly say that I have ever spoken as your friend. You know what hostile criticism your work sometimes evokes here,[1] and I wage a perpetual war with many friends on your behalf. But I am glad to say that I have been the means of making your work known to many who were scoffers at first.[2] The years which have passed have not been uneventful to me, and I have felt and thought and suffered much in them, and I can truly say that from you I have had much pleasure and much consolation—and I do believe that your open earnest speech has not been thrown away on me or that my life and thought fail to be marked with its impress. I write this openly because I feel that with you one must be open. We have just had tonight a hot debate on your genius at the Fortnightly Club in which I had the privilege of putting forward my views—I think with success.

Do not think me cheeky for writing this. I only hope we may sometime meet[3] and I shall be able perhaps to say what I cannot write. Dowden promised to get me a copy of your new edition and I hope that for any other work which you may have you will let me always be an early subscriber. I am sorry that you're not strong. Many of

---

1 This is referring to Whitman's poetry collection, *Leaves of Grass*. Its readers were outraged at the blatant portrayal of sexuality in the poems, which eventually led to its ban.

2 Bram Stoker's devotion to Whitman was apparent to his peers at Trinity College, where he read, discussed, and even defended Whitman's works.

3 Bram Stoker met Walt Whitman thrice between 1884 and 1887.

us are hoping to see you in Ireland. We had arranged to have a meeting for you. I do not know if you like getting letters. If you do I shall only be too happy to send you news of how thought goes among the men I know. With truest wishes for your health and happiness believe me,

Your friend

Bram Stoker

You Are Passing Through a Darkness

Henry James' letter to Grace Norton, written c. 1883

131 Mount Vernon St.,
Boston

July 28th

My dear Grace,

Before the sufferings of others I am always utterly powerless, and the letter you gave me reveals such depths of suffering that I hardly know what to say to you.[1] This indeed is not my last word—but it must be my first. You are not isolated, verily, in such states of feeling as this—that is, in the sense that you appear to

---

1 Grace Norton had informed James in a letter of how a death in her family had been depressing her. Norton had, perhaps, asked for James' advice since James too had suffered from it at a point in his life, so much so that, allegedly, his brother had requested the famous psychologist, Sigmund Freud, to pay James a visit.

make all the misery of all mankind your own; only I have a terrible sense that you give all and receive nothing—that there is no reciprocity in your sympathy—that you have all the affliction of it and none of the returns. However—I am determined not to speak to you except with the voice of stoicism.

I don't know why we live—the gift of life comes to us from I don't know what source or for what purpose; but I believe we can go on living for the reason that (always of course up to a certain point) life is the most valuable thing we know anything about and it is therefore presumptively a great mistake to surrender it while there is any yet left in the cup. In other words consciousness is an illimitable power, and though at times it may seem to be all consciousness of misery, yet in the way it propagates itself from wave to wave, so that we never cease to feel, though at moments we appear to, try to, pray to, there is something that holds one in one's place, makes it a standpoint in the universe which it is probably good not to forsake. You are right in your consciousness that we are all echoes and reverberations of the *same*, and you are noble when your interest and pity as to everything that surrounds you, appears to have a sustaining and harmonizing power. Only don't, I beseech you, *generalize* too much in these sympathies and tendernesses—remember that every life is a special problem which is not yours but another's, and content yourself with the terrible algebra of your own. Don't melt too much into the universe, but be as solid and dense and fixed as you can. We all live together, and those of us who love and know, live so most. We help each other—even unconsciously, each in our own effort, we lighten the effort of others, we contribute to the sum of success, make it possible for others to live. Sorrow comes in great waves—no one can know that better than you—but it rolls over us, and though it may almost smother us it leaves us on the spot and we know that if it is strong we are stronger, inasmuch as it passes and we remain. It wears us, uses us, but we wear it and use it in return; and it is blind, whereas we after a manner see.

My dear Grace, you are passing through a darkness in which I myself in my ignorance see nothing but that you have been made wretchedly ill by it; but it is only a darkness, it is not an end, or *the* end. Don't think, don't feel, any more than you can help, don't conclude or decide—don't do anything but *wait.* Everything will pass, and serenity and *accepted* mysteries and disillusionments, and the tenderness of a few good people, and new opportunities and ever so much of life, in a word, will remain. You will do all sorts of things yet, and I will help you. The only thing is not to *melt* in the meanwhile. I insist upon the necessity of a sort of mechanical condensation—so that however fast the horse may run away there will, when he pulls up, be a somewhat agitated but perfectly identical

G. N. left in the saddle. Try not to be ill—that is all; for in that there is a future. You are marked out for success, and you must not fail. You have my tenderest affection and all my confidence.

Ever your faithful friend—

Henry James

Our Filthy Job as Painters

Vincent Van Gogh and Paul Gauguin's joint letter to Emile Bernard, dated 1888

My dear old Bernard,

We've done a great deal of work these past few days, and in the meantime I've read Zola's Le rêve,[1] so I've hardly had time to write.

Gauguin[2] interests me greatly as a man — greatly. For a long time it has seemed to me that in our filthy job as painters[3] we have the greatest need of people with the hands and stomach of a

---

1 Emily Zola's *Le Reve* was published in that year. It is about an orphaned girl who falls for a nobleman.

2 Paul Gauguin was a post-Impressionist artist, whose work was appreciated after his death. Impressionism was a subset of the Modernist movement in painting. It developed in 1860's in Paris, spread in Europe, and then reached the United States. The key feature of art in impressionism was to capture the real, instead of the ideal, and to canvass an ephemeral moment, an impression.

3 Not only filthy, Van Gogh's career as a painter did not turn out to be lucrative at all. He sold only one painting in his lifetime.

labourer. More natural tastes — more amorous and benevolent temperaments — than the decadent and exhausted Parisian man-about-town.

Now here, without the slightest doubt, we're in the presence of an unspoiled creature with the instincts of a wild beast. With Gauguin, blood and sex have the edge over ambition. But enough of that, you've seen him close at hand longer than I have, just wanted to tell you first impressions in a few words.

Next, I don't think it will astonish you greatly if I tell you that our discussions are tending to deal with the terrific subject of an association of certain painters. Ought or may this association have a commercial character, yes or no? We haven't reached any result yet, and haven't so much as set foot on a new continent yet. Now I, who have a presentiment of a new world, who certainly believe in the possibility of a great renaissance of art. Who believe that this new art will have the tropics for its homeland.

It seems to me that we ourselves are serving only as intermediaries. And that it will only be a subsequent generation that will succeed in living in peace. Anyway, all that, our duties and our possibilities for action could become clearer to us only through actual experience.

I was a little surprised not yet to have received the studies that you promised in exchange for mine.

Now something that will interest you — we've made some excursions in the brothels, and it's likely that we'll eventually go there often to work. At the moment Gauguin has a canvas in progress of the same night café that I also painted,[4] but with figures seen in the brothels. It promises to become a beautiful thing.

I've made two studies of falling leaves in an avenue of poplars, and a third study of the whole of this avenue, entirely yellow.

I declare I don't understand why I don't do figure studies, while theoretically it's sometimes so difficult for me to imagine the painting of the future as anything other than a new series of powerful portraitists, simple and comprehensible to the whole of the general public. Anyway, perhaps I'll soon get down to doing brothels.

---

4 *The Night Café* had been inspired by the settings of a brothel that Van Gogh had visited. Shortly after he finished the painting, Paul Gauguin had come to live with him, and then had started on his own version of the same painting.

I'll leave a page for Gauguin, who will probably also write to you, and I shake your hand firmly in thought.

Ever yours,
Vincent

Milliet the 2nd lieut. Zouaves has left for Africa, and would be very glad if you were to write to him one of these days.

[*Continued by Paul Gauguin*]

You will indeed do well to write him what your intentions are, so that he could take steps beforehand to prepare the way for you.

Mr Milliet, *second lieutenant of Zouaves*, Guelma, Africa.

Don't listen to Vincent; as you know, he's prone to admire and ditto to be indulgent. His idea about the future of a new generation in the tropics seems absolutely right to me as a painter, and I still intend going back there when I find the funds. A little bit of luck, who knows?

Vincent has done two studies of falling leaves in an avenue, which are in my room and which you would like very much. On very coarse, but very good sacking.

Send news of yourself and of all the pals.

Yours,
Paul Gauguin

Catch Me When You Can

Jack the Ripper's[1] letter to George Lusk, written on 15 October, 1888

From hell.

Mr Lusk,[2]
Sor
I send you half the Kidne[3] I took from one woman prasarved it for you tother piece I fried and ate it was very nise. I may send you the bloody knif that took it out if you only wate a whil longer
signed
Catch me when you can Mishter Lusk

---

1 Nobody knows whether this letter was from the actual murderer or someone who was falsely claiming to be him.

2 George Lusk was the chairman of the Whitechapel Vigilance Committee in 1888.

3 Jack the Ripper is known to have killed at least five prostitutes. It is conjectured that he had knowledge of the human anatomy since he mutilated the bodies of his victims almost with surgical precision.

I Was Satisfied and Happy

Helen Keller's letter to Sarah Fuller

South Boston, Mass.,
April 3, 1890

My dear Miss Fuller,[1]
My heart is full of joy this beautiful morning, because I have learned to speak many new words, and I can make a few sentences.[2] Last evening I went out in the yard and spoke to the moon. I said, "O! moon come to me!" Do you think the lovely moon was glad that I could speak to her? How glad my mother will be. I can hardly wait for June to come I am so eager to speak to her and to my precious little sister. Mildred could not understand me when I spelled with my fingers, but now she will sit in my lap and I will tell her many things to please her, and we shall be so happy together. Are you very, very happy

---

1 Sarah Fuller was the principal of Horace Mann School for Deaf.

2 Helen Keller had contracted an illness a year and a half after her birth that left her blind and deaf.

because you can make so many people happy? I think you are very kind and patient, and I love you very dearly. My teacher told me Tuesday that you wanted to know how I came to wish to talk with my mouth. I will tell you all about it, for I remember my thoughts perfectly. When I was a very little child I used to sit in my mother's lap all the time, because I was very timid, and did not like to be left by myself. And I would keep my little hand on her face all the while, because it amused me to feel her face and lips move when she talked with people. I did not know then what she was doing, for I was quite ignorant of all things. Then when I was older I learned to play with my nurse and the little negro children and I noticed that they kept moving their lips just like my mother, so I moved mine too, but sometimes it made me angry and I would hold my playmates' mouths very hard. I did not know then that it was very naughty to do so. After a long time my dear teacher came to me, and taught me to communicate with my fingers and I was satisfied and happy.[3] But when I came to school in Boston I met some deaf people who talked with their mouths like all other people, and one

---

3 Anne Sullivan, the woman who taught Helen Keller how to read, write, and communicate. By placing her fingers on the person's lips, Keller determined the letters spoken by determining the way their lips moved. 'The position of the hand is as easy to feel as it is to see. I do not feel each letter any more than you see each letter separately when you read.' (From *The Story of my Life*)

day a lady who had been to Norway came to see me, and told me of a blind and deaf girl she had seen in that far away land who had been taught to speak and understand others when they spoke to her.[4] This good and happy news delighted me exceedingly, for then I was sure that I should learn also. I tried to make sounds like my little playmates, but teacher told me that the voice was very delicate and sensitive and that it would injure it to make incorrect sounds, and promised to take me to see a kind and wise lady who would teach me rightly.

That lady was yourself. Now I am as happy as the little birds, because I can speak and perhaps I shall sing too. All of my friends will be so surprised and glad.

Your loving little pupil,
HELEN A. KELLER.

---

4 Knowing about this girl in Norway, who had the same disabilities as Helen, had further fueled her motivation to be able to speak like a normal person.

Flight Is Possible to Man

Wilbur Wright's letter to Octave Chanute

Wright Cycle Company
1127 West Third Street
DAYTON, OHIO, May 13, 1900

Mr. Octave Chanute, Esq.
Chicago, Ill.

Dear Sir;

For some years I have been afflicted with the belief that flight is possible to man.[1] My disease has increased in severity and I feel that it will soon cost me an increased amount of money if not my life. I have been trying to arrange my affairs in such a way that I can devote my entire time for a few months to experiment in this field.

---

1 Three years after writing this letter, Wilbur Wright, with his brother Orville, piloted the first flying machine in North Carolina.

My general ideas of the subject are similar to those held by most practical experimenters, to wit: that what is chiefly needed is skill rather than machinery. The flight of the buzzard and similar sailors is a convincing demonstration of the value of skill, and the partial needlessness of motors. It is possible to fly without motors, but not without knowledge & skill. This I conceive to be fortunate, for man, by reason of his greater intellect, can more reasonably hope to equal birds in knowledge, than to equal nature in the perfection of her machinery.

Assuming then that Lilienthal was correct in his ideas of the principles on which man should proceed, I conceive that his failure was due chiefly to the inadequacy of his method, and of his apparatus. As to his method, the fact that in five years' time he spent only about five hours, altogether, in actual flight is sufficient to show that his method was inadequate. Even the simplest intellectual or acrobatic feats could never be learned with so short practice, and even Methuselah could never have become an expert stenographer with one hour per year for practice. I also conceive Lilienthal's apparatus to be inadequate not only from the fact that he failed, but my observations of the flight of birds convince me that birds use more positive and energetic methods of regaining equilibrium than that of shifting the center of gravity.

With this general statement of my principles and belief I will proceed to describe the plan and apparatus it is my intention to test. In explaining these, my object is to learn to what extent similar plans have been tested and found to be failures, and also to obtain such suggestions as your great knowledge and experience might enable you to give me. I make no secret of my plans for the reason that I believe no financial profit will accrue to the inventor of the first flying machine, and that only those who are willing to give as well as to receive suggestions can hope to link their names with the honor of its discovery. The problem is too great for one man alone and unaided to solve in secret.

My plan then is this. I shall in a suitable locality erect a light tower about one hundred and fifty feet high. A rope passing over a pulley at the top will serve as a sort of kite string. It will be so counterbalanced that when the rope is drawn out one hundred & fifty feet it will sustain a pull equal to the weight of the operator and apparatus or nearly so. The wind will blow the machine out from the base of the tower and the weight will be sustained partly by the upward pull of the rope and partly by the lift of the wind. The counterbalance will be so arranged that the pull decreases as the line becomes shorter and ceases entirely when its length has been decreased to one hundred feet. The aim will be to eventually practice in a wind capable of sustaining the operator at a height equal to the top of the tower. The pull of the rope will take the place of a motor in counteracting drift. I see, of course, that the pull of the rope will introduce complications which are not met in free flight, but if the plan will only enable me to remain in the air for practice by the hour instead of by the second, I hope to acquire skill sufficient to overcome both these difficulties and those inherent to flight. Knowledge and skill in handling the machine are absolute essentials to flight and it is impossible to obtain them without extensive practice.

The method employed by Mr. Pilcher of towing with horses in many respects is better than that I propose to employ, but offers no guarantee that the experimenter will escape accident long enough to acquire skill sufficient to prevent accident. In my plan I rely on the rope and counterbalance to at least break the force of a fall. My observation of the flight of buzzards leads me to believe that they regain their lateral balance, when partly overturned by a gust of wind, by a torsion of the tips of the wings. If the rear edge of the right wing tip is twisted upward and the left downward the bird becomes an animated windmill and instantly begins to turn, a line from its head to its tail being the axis. It thus regains its level even if thrown on its beam ends, so to speak, as I have frequently seen them. I think the bird also in general retains its lateral equilibrium, partly by presenting its two wings at different angles to the wind, and partly by drawing in one wing, thus reducing its area.

I incline to the belief that the first is the more important and usual method.

In the apparatus I intend to employ I make use of the torsion principle. In appearance it is very similar to the "double-deck" machine with which the experiments of yourself and Mr. Herring were conducted in 1896-7. The point on which it differs in principle is that the cross-stays which prevent the upper plane from moving forward and backward are removed, and each end of the upper plane is independently moved forward or backward with respect to the lower plane by a suitable lever or other arrangement. By this plan the whole upper plane may be moved forward or backward, to attain longitudinal equilibrium, by moving both hands forward or backward together. Lateral equilibrium is gained by moving one end more than the other or by moving them in opposite directions. If you will make a square cardboard tube two inches in diameter and eight or ten long and choose two sides for your planes you will at once see the torsional effect of moving one end of the upper plane forward and the other backward, and how this effect is attained without sacrificing lateral stiffness. My plan is to attach the tail rigidly to the rear upright stays which connect the planes, the effect of which will be that when the upper plane is thrown forward the end of the tail is elevated, so that the tail assists gravity in restoring longitudinal balance.

My experiments hitherto with this apparatus have been confined to machines spreading about fifteen square feet of surface, and have been sufficiently encouraging to induce me to lay plans for a trial with a full-sized machine. My business requires that my experimental work be confined to the months between September and January and I would be particularly thankful for advice as to a suitable locality where I could depend on winds of about fifteen miles per hour without rain or too inclement weather. I am certain that such localities are rare.

I have your Progress in Flying Machines and your articles in the Annuals of '95,'96, & '97, as also your recent articles in the Independent. If you can give me information as to where an account of Pilcher's experiments can be obtained I would greatly appreciate your kindness.[2]

Yours truly,

Wilbur Wright

---

2 Four days later, Octave Chanute had responded to Wright's letter, guiding him and suggesting locations where Wright might begin gliding. Impressed with their ideas, he continued advising the Wright brothers, his correspondence with them ending with his death.

True Manliness of Character

Theodore Roosevelt's letter to Kermit Roosevelt

White House, Oct. 2, 1903.

DEAR KERMIT:

I was very glad to get your letter. Am glad you are playing football. I should be very sorry to see either you or Ted devoting most of your attention to athletics, and I haven't got any special ambition to see you shine overmuch in athletics at college, at least (if you go there), because I think it tends to take up too much time; but I do like to feel that you are manly and able to hold your own in rough, hardy sports. I would rather have a boy of mine stand high in his studies than high in athletics, but I could a great deal rather have him show true manliness of character than show either intellectual or physical prowess; and I believe you and Ted both bid fair to develop just such character.

There! you will think this a dreadfully preaching letter! I suppose I have a natural tendency to preach just at present because I am overwhelmed with my work. I enjoy being President, and I like to do the work and have my hand on the lever. But it is very worrying and puzzling, and I have to make up my mind to accept every kind of attack and misrepresentation. It is a great comfort to me to read the life and letters of Abraham Lincoln. I am more and more impressed every day, not only with the man's wonderful power and sagacity, but with his literally endless patience, and at the same time his unflinching resolution.

You Are a Wonderful Creature

Mark Twain's letter to Helen Keller

Riverdale-on-the-Hudson
St. Patrick's Day, '03

Dear Helen,—

I *must* steal half a moment from my work to say how glad I am to have your book,[1] and how highly I value it, both for its own sake and as a remembrance of an affectionate friendship which has subsisted between us for nine years without a break,[2] and without a single act of violence that I can call to mind. I suppose there is nothing like it in heaven; and not likely to be, until we get there and show off. I often think of it with longing, and how they'll say, "There they

---

1 The book Mark Twain is referring to is the autobiography of Helen Keller, *The Story of My Life.* H H Rogers had offered his financial assistance to Keller on Twain's suggestion. This had enabled her to complete her education and write her first book.

2 They met each other for the first time in 1895 at New York.

come—sit down in front!" I am practicing with a tin halo. You do the same. I was at Henry Roger's last night, and of course we talked of you. He is not at all well;—you will not like to hear that; but like you and me, he is just as lovely as ever.

I am charmed with your book—enchanted. You are a wonderful creature, the most wonderful in the world—you and your other half together—Miss Sullivan, I mean, for it took the pair of you to make a complete and perfect whole. How she stands out in her letters! her brilliancy, penetration, originality, wisdom, character, and the fine literary competencies of her pen—they are all there.

Oh, dear me, how unspeakably funny and owlishly idiotic and grotesque was that "plagiarism" farce![3] As if there was much of anything in any human utterance, oral or written, *except* plagiarism! The kernel, the soul—let us go further and say the substance, the bulk, the actual and valuable material of *all* human utterances—is plagiarism. For substantially all ideas are second-hand,

---

3 The 'plagiarism farce' refers to the controversy that had surrounded one of the stories written by Keller, namely, 'The Frost King'. Keller had sent it to Michael Anagmos, head of the Perkins School for Blind, who published it in *The Mentor.* Later, it came to light that this story had many similarities to Margaret T. Canby's 'The Frost Fairies', and Keller was charged with plagiarism.

consciously and unconsciously drawn from a million outside sources, and daily use by the garnerer with a pride and satisfaction born of the superstition that he originated them; whereas there is not a rag of originality about them anywhere except the little discoloration they get from his mental and moral calibre and his temperament, and which is revealed in characteristics of phrasing. When a great orator makes a great speech you are listening to ten centuries and ten thousand men—but we call it *his* speech, and really some exceedingly small portion of it *is* his. But not enough to signify. It is merely a Waterloo. It is Wellington's battle, in some degree, and we call it his; but there are others that contributed. It takes a thousand men to invent a telegraph, or a steam engine, or a phonograph, or a telephone or any other important thing—and the last man gets the credit and we forget the others. He added his little *mite*—that is all he did. These object lessons should teach us that ninety-nine parts of all things that proceed from the intellect are plagiarisms, pure and simple; and the lesson ought to make us modest. But nothing can do that.

Then why don't we unwittingly reproduce the *phrasing* of a story, as well as the story itself? It can hardly happen—to the extent of fifty words except in the case of a child; its memory-tablet is not lumbered with impressions, and the actual language can have graving-room there, and preserve the language a year or two, but a grown person's memory-tablet is a palimpsest, with hardly a bare space upon which to engrave a phrase. It must be a very rare thing that a whole page gets so sharply printed on a man's mind, by a single reading, that it will stay long enough to turn up some time or other to be mistaken by him for his own. No doubt we are constantly littering our literature with *disconnected* sentences borrowed from books at some unremembered time and now imagined to be our own, but that is about the most we can do. In 1866 I read Dr. Holmes's poems, in the Sandwich Islands. A year and a half later I stole his dedication, without knowing it, and used it to dedicate my "Innocents Abroad" with. Then years afterward I was talking with Dr. Holmes about it. He was not an ignorant ass—no, not he; he was not a collection of decayed human turnips, like your "Plagiarism Court;" and so when I said, "I know now where I stole it, but whom did you steal it from," he said, "I don't remember; I only know I stole it from somebody, because I have never originated anything altogether myself, nor met anyone who had."

To think of those solemn donkeys breaking a little child's heart with their ignorant rubbish about plagiarism! I couldn't sleep for blaspheming about it last night. Why, their whole lives, their whole histories, all their learning, all their thoughts, all their opinions were one solid rock of plagiarism, and they didn't know it and never suspected it. A gang of dull and hoary pirates piously setting themselves the task of disciplining and purifying a kitten that they think they've caught filching a chop! Oh, dam—

But you finish it, dear, I am running short of vocabulary today.

Ever lovingly your friend

Mark

A Writer Is Not a Literary Bureau

Jack London's letter to an aspiring writer

Oakland, California
Febraury 20, 1905

Dear Sir:

Every time a writer tells the truth about a manuscript (or book), to a friend-author, he loses that friend, or sees that friendship dim and fade away to a ghost of what it was formerly.

Every time a writer tells the truth about a manuscript (or book), to a stranger-author, he makes an enemy.

If the writer loves his friend and fears to lose him, he lies to his friend.

But what's the good of straining himself to lie to strangers?

And, with like insistence, what's the good of making enemies anyway?

Furthermore, a known writer is overwhelmed by requests from strangers to read their work and pass judgment upon it. This is properly the work of a literary bureau. A writer is not a literary bureau. If he is foolish enough to become a literary bureau, he will cease to be a writer. He won't have time to write.

Also, as a charitable literary bureau, he will receive no pay. Wherefore he will soon go bankrupt and himself live upon the charity of friends (if he has not already made them all his enemies by telling them the truth), while he will behold his wife and children went their melancholy way to the poorhouse.

Sympathy for the struggling unknown is all very well. It is beautiful—but there are so many struggling unknowns, something like several millions of them. And sympathy can be worked too hard. Sympathy begins at home. The writer would far rather allow the multitudinous unknowns to remain unknown than to allow his near and dear ones to occupy pauper pallets and potter's fields.

Sincerely yours,

Jack London

An Idiot of the 33rd Degree

Mark Twain's letter to J H Todd

Nov. 20. 1905

J. H. Todd
1212 Webster St.
San Francisco, Cal.

Dear Sir,

Your letter is an insoluble puzzle to me. The handwriting is good and exhibits considerable character, and there are even traces of intelligence in what you say, yet the letter and the accompanying advertisements profess to be the work of the same hand. The person who wrote the advertisements is without doubt the most ignorant person now alive on the planet; also without doubt he is an idiot, an idiot of the 33rd degree,[1] and scion of an ancestral procession

---

1 Mark Twain had received a letter, with a pamphlet, from J H Todd. He was attempting to sell him a medicine called The Elixir of Life that could, allegedly, cure fatal diseases such as meningitis and diphtheria. Realizing that the medicine was obviously a fake, Twain's temper might not have flared enough to pen down such an insulting response had it not been for the fact that his son and daughter died after contracting the diseases that the medicine boasted of curing.

of idiots stretching back to the Missing Link. It puzzles me to make out how the same hand could have constructed your letter and your advertisements. Puzzles fret me, puzzles annoy me, puzzles exasperate me; and always, for a moment, they arouse in me an unkind state of mind toward the person who has puzzled me. A few moments from now my resentment will have faded and passed and I shall probably even be praying for you; but while there is yet time I hasten to wish that you may take a dose of your own poison by mistake, and enter swiftly into the damnation which you and all other patent medicine assassins have so remorselessly earned and do so richly deserve.

Adieu, adieu, adieu!

Mark Twain

I Cherish an Unappeasable Bitterness

Mark Twain's letter to Asa Don Dickinson

21 FIFTH AVENUE,
November 21, 1905

DEAR SIR:

I am greatly troubled by what you say.[1] I wrote Tom Sawyer and Huck Finn for adults exclusively, and it always distresses me when I find that boys and girls have been allowed access to them. The mind that becomes soiled in youth can never again be washed clean; I know this by my own experience, and to this day I cherish an

---

1 Twain is referring to the ban that had been placed on his book *The Adventures of Huckleberry Finn*. The language of the book was deemed immoral and racist, since the word had ben used to refer to African-American characters. Naturally, the abolitionists were furious, but so were the others in America. The novel portrayed friendship between a black man and a white boy at a time when majority of the American society frowned upon such co-mingling among people of difference races.

unappeasable bitterness against the unfaithful guardians of my young life, who not only permitted but compelled me to read an unexpurgated Bible through before I was 15 years old. None can do that and ever draw a clean sweet breath again this side of the grave. Ask that young lady—she will tell you so.

Most honestly do I wish I could say a softening word or two in defence of Huck's character,[2] since you wish it, but really in my opinion it is no better than those of Solomon, David, Satan, and the rest of the sacred brotherhood.

If there is an unexpurgated Bible in the Children's Department, won't you please help that young woman remove Huck and Tom from that questionable companionship?

Sincerely yours,

(Signed, 'S. L. Clemens')[3]

I shall not show your letter to anyone—it is safe with me.

---

2 The Brooklyn Public Library had banned *The Adventures of Huckleberry Finn*, claiming that Huck, the protagonist, lacked manners and exhibited inappropriate behaviour.

3 Samuel Langhorne Clemens was Mark Twain's real name.

Dickens' Characters

Theodore Roosevelt's letter to Ted Roosevelt

White House, May 20, 1906.

DEAR TED:

Mother read us your note and I was interested in the discussion between you and ——— over Dickens. Dickens' characters are really to a great extent personified attributes rather than individuals. In consequence, while there are not nearly as many who are actually like people one meets, as for instance in Thackeray, there are a great many more who possess *characteristics* which we encounter continually, though rarely as strongly developed as in the fictional originals. So Dickens' characters last almost as Bunyan's do. For instance, Jefferson Brick and Elijah Pogram and Hannibal Chollop are all real personifications of certain bad tendencies in American life, and I am continually thinking of or alluding to some newspaper editor or Senator or homicidal rowdy by one of these three names. I never met any one exactly like Uriah Heep, but now and then we see individuals show traits which make it easy to describe them, with reference to those traits, as Uriah Heep. It is just the same with Micawber. Mrs. Nickleby is not quite a real person, but she typifies, in accentuated form, traits which a great many real persons possess, and I am continually thinking of her when I meet them. There are half a dozen books of Dickens which have, I think, furnished more characters which are the constant companions of the ordinary educated man around us, than is true of any other half-dozen volumes published within the same period.

In the Interest of Truth

M K Gandhi's letter to Leo Tolstoy

Westminster Palace Hotel,

4, Victoria Street,

London, S.W.,

1st October, 1909

SIR,

I take the liberty of inviting your attention to what has been going on in the Transvaal (South Africa) for nearly three years.

There is in that colony a British Indian population of nearly 13,000. These Indians have for several years laboured under the various legal disabilities. The prejudice against colour and in some respect against Asiatics is intense in that colony It is largely due, so far as Asiatics are concerned, to trade jealousy.

The climax was reached three years ago, with a law[1] which I and many others considered to be degrading and calculated to unman those to whom it was applicable.

I felt that submission to law of this nature was inconsistent with the spirit of true religion. I and some of my friends were and still are firm believers in the doctrine of non-resistance to evil. I had the privilege of studying your writings also, which left a deep impression on my mind. British Indians, before whom the position was fully explained, accepted the advice that we should not submit to the legislation, but that we should suffer imprisonment, or whatever other penalties the law may impose for its breach. The result has been that nearly one-half of the Indian population that was unable to stand the heat of the struggle, to suffer the hardships of imprisonment, have withdrawn from the Transvaal rather than submit to law which they have considered degrading. Of the other half, nearly 2,500 have for conscience's sake allowed themselves to be imprisoned, some as many as five times. The imprisonments have varied from four days to six months; in the majority

---

1 This was the Asiatic Law Amendment Ordinance that was passed in Transvaal in August 1906. Also known as the Black Act, it mandated that all Indians were to register with the registrar of Asiatics. If found without a registration certificate, Indians could be fined, imprisoned, or even deported.

of cases with hard labour. Many have been financially ruined.

At present there are over hundred passive resisters in the Transvaal goals. Some of these have been very poor men, earning their livelihood from day to day. The result has been that their wives and children have had to be supported out of public contributions, also largely raised from passive resisters.

This has put a severe strain upon British Indians, but in my opinion they have risen to the occasion. The struggle still continues and one does not know when the end will come. This, however, some of us at least have seen most clearly, that passive resistance will and can succeed where brute force must fail. We also notice that in so far as the struggle has been prolonged, it has been due largely to our weakness, and hence to a belief having been engendered in the mind of the Government that we would not be able to stand continued suffering.

Together with a friend, I have come here to see the imperial authorities and to place before them the position, with a view to seeking redress. Passive resisters have recognized that they should have nothing to do with pleading with the Government, but the deputation has come at the instance of the weaker members of the community, and it therefore represents their weakness rather than their strength. But in the course of my observation here, I have felt that if a general competition for an essay on the Ethics and Efficacy of Passive Resistance were invited, it would popularize the movement and make people think. A friend has raised the question of morality in connection with the proposed competition. He thinks that such an invitation would be inconsistent with the true spirit of passive resistance, and that it would amount to buying opinion. May I ask you to favour me with your opinion on the subject of morality? And if you consider that there is nothing wrong in inviting contributions, I would ask you also to give me the names of those whom I should specially approach to write upon the subject.

There is one thing more, with reference to which I would trespass upon your time. A copy of your letter addressed to a Hindu[2] on the present unrest in India has been placed in my hands by a friend. On the face of it, it appears to represent your views. It is the intention of my friend, at his own expense, to have 20,000 copies printed and distributed and to have it translated also. We have, however, not been able to secure the original, and we

---

2 Gandhi, a stringent propagator of non-violence, admired Tolstoy's policy of non-resistance. Reading Tolstoy's *A Letter to a Hindu*, he was impressed and, perhaps, glad that Tolstoy's views on the matter mirrored his own. The letter proclaimed that peaceful resistance was the only proper way for India to gain independence.

do not feel justified in printing it, unless we are sure of the accuracy of the copy and of the fact that it is your letter. I venture to enclose herewith a copy of the copy, and should esteem it a favour if you kindly let me know whether it is your letter, whether it is an accurate copy and whether you approve of its publication in the above manner. If you will add anything further to the letter please do so.

I would also venture to make a suggestion. In the concluding paragraph you seem to dissuade the reader from the belief in reincarnation. I do not know whether (if it is not impertinent on my part to mention this) you have specially studied the question. Reincarnation or transmigration is a cherished belief with millions in India, indeed in China also. With many one might almost say it is a matter of experience, no longer a matter of academic acceptance. It explains reasonably the many mysteries of life. With some of the passive resisters who have gone through the gaols of the Transvaal, it has been their solace. My object in writing this is not to convince you of the truth of the doctrine, but to ask you if you will please remove the word "reincarnation" from the other things you have dissuaded your reader from.

In the letter in question you have quoted largely from Krishna and given reference to passages. I should thank you to give me the title of the book from which the quotations have been made. I have wearied you with this letter. I am aware that those who honour you and endeavour to follow you have no right to trespass upon your time, but it is rather their duty to refrain from giving you trouble, so far as possible. I have, however, who am an utter stranger to you, taken the liberty of addressing this communication in the interests of truth, and in order to have your advice on problems, the solution of which you have made your life work.

With respects, I remain,

Your obedient servant,

M. K GANDHI

One of the Leading Theoreticians of the Future

Albert Einstein's recommendation letter, by Marie Curie

Paris, November 17, 1911

Dear Sir,

I have just received your letter, in which you asked for my personal impression of Mr. Einstein, whom I recently had the pleasure to meet. You also say that Mr. Einstein wishes very much to return to Zurich and could soon have the opportunity to do so.

I have often admired the papers published by Mr. Einstein on issues dealing with modern theoretical physics. Moreover, I believe that theoretical physicists agree that these papers are of the highest order. In Brussels, where I participated in a scientific conference in which Mr. Einstein also took part, I was able to appreciate the clarity of his mind, the extent of his documentation and the depth of his knowledge. If we consider that Mr. Einstein is still very young, we are right to have great hope in him, and to see him as one of the leading theoreticians of the future. I think that the scientific institution willing to give Mr. Einstein the work he desires, either by appointing him an existing chair or by creating for him the chair in the conditions he deserves, could be greatly honored by such a decision and would certainly be providing a great service to science.

If, by offering my opinion, I could by a small measure contribute to the solution desired by Mr. Einstein,[1] I would be extremely pleased.

Accept, I beg of you, dear Sir, the assurance of my best wishes.

M. Curie

Faculty of Sciences, Paris
(General Physics Laboratory)

---

1 Einstein had applied for the position of Professor of Theoretical Physics at the Swiss Federal Institute of Technology. He was hired by the institute and worked there till 1914, after which he left for Berlin.

I Want to Thank You

Thomas Edison's letter to Henry Ford

From the Laboratory of Thomas A. Edison

Orange N.J. Feb. 13th. 1915

Mr. Henry Ford.
Detroit, Hich.

My dear Mr. Ford:

Let me thank you for the sixty-eight thousand congratulations that you sent me for birthday yesterday, and also for all your good wishes. It was all very cheering to me, and I want to thank you all very much.

We are making great progress around here. Everything is booming. We are making about twenty thousand cylinder records a day and some six or seven thousand disc records daily, and a large number of mechanisms for machines. We have developed an entirely new model of Disc Machine, which has been completed within sixty days, including tools, jigs etc., for its manufacture, and we are now shipping them out to customers. The Storage Battery business is picking up. I had a telegram from the Secretary of the Navy yesterday telling me he had just signed the order for a set of our batteries for a new submarine, ($90,000) and had reported to me later in the day that a large order was coming our way for use with the wireless.

These and other cheering items were quite sufficient to make my birthday a pleasant one to remember.

With kindest regards to you all, I remain

Your very truly,
(Signed Thomas A. Edison)

Delivering Mankind from the Menace of War

Albert Einstein's letter to Sigmund Freud, written in 1932

Dear Mr. Freud: The proposal of the League of Nations and its International Institute of Intellectual Cooperation at Paris that I should invite a person, to be chosen by myself, to a frank exchange of views on any problem that I might select affords me a very welcome opportunity of conferring with you upon a question which, as things now are, seems the most insistent of all the problems civilization has to face. This is the problem: Is there any way of delivering mankind from the menace of war?[1] It is common knowledge that, with the advance of modern science, this issue has come to mean a matter of life and death for Civilization as we know it; nevertheless, for all the zeal displayed, every attempt at its solution has ended in a lamentable breakdown.

---

1 Einstein had, inadvertently, played a pivotal role in ushering in the atomic age through his letter to Franklin Roosevelt during the Second World War, which had made possible the detonation of the first nuclear weapons in the United States.

I believe, moreover, that those whose duty it is to tackle the problem professionally and practically are growing only too aware of their impotence to deal with it, and have now a very lively desire to learn the views of men who, absorbed in the pursuit of science, can see world problems in the perspective distance lends. As for me, the normal objective of my thought affords no insight into the dark places of human will and feeling. Thus, in the inquiry now proposed, I can do little more than to seek to clarify the question at issue and, clearing the ground of the more obvious solutions, enable you to bring the light of your far-reaching knowledge of man's instinctive life to bear upon the problem. There are certain psychological obstacles whose existence a layman in the mental sciences may dimly surmise, but whose interrelations and vagaries he is incompetent to fathom; you, I am convinced, will be able to suggest educative methods, lying more or less outside the scope of politics, which will eliminate these obstacles.

As one immune from nationalist bias, I personally see a simple way of dealing with the superficial (i.e., administrative) aspect of the problem: the setting up, by international consent, of a legislative and judicial body to settle every conflict arising between nations. Each nation would undertake to abide by the orders issued by this legislative body, to invoke its decision in every dispute, to accept its judgments unreservedly and to carry out every measure the tribunal deems necessary for the execution of its decrees. But here, at the outset, I come up against a difficulty; a tribunal is a human institution which, in proportion as the power at its disposal is inadequate to enforce its verdicts, is all the more prone to suffer these to be deflected by extrajudicial pressure. This is a fact with which we have to reckon; law and might inevitably go hand in hand, and juridical decisions approach more nearly the ideal justice demanded by the community (in whose name and interests these verdicts are pronounced) insofar as the community has effective power to compel respect of its juridical ideal. But at present we are far from possessing any supranational organization competent to render verdicts of incontestable authority and enforce absolute submission to the execution of its verdicts. Thus I am led to my first axiom: The quest of international security involves the unconditional surrender by every nation, in a certain measure, of its liberty of action–its sovereignty that is to say–and it is clear beyond all doubt that no other road can lead to such security.

The ill success, despite their obvious sincerity, of all the efforts made during the last decade to reach this goal leaves us no room to doubt that strong psychological factors are at work which paralyze these efforts. Some of these factors are not far to seek. The craving for power which characterizes the governing class in every nation is hostile to any limitation of the national sovereignty.

This political power hunger is often supported by the activities of another group, whose aspirations are on purely mercenary, economic lines. I have especially in mind that small but determined group, active in every nation, composed of individuals who, indifferent to social considerations and restraints, regard warfare, the manufacture and sale of arms, simply as an occasion to advance their personal interests and enlarge their personal authority.

But recognition of this obvious fact is merely the first step toward an appreciation of the actual state of affairs. Another question follows hard upon it: How is it possible for this small clique to bend the will of the majority, who stand to lose and suffer by a state of war, to the service of their ambitions. An obvious answer to this question would seem to be that the minority, the ruling class at present, has the schools and press, usually the Church as well, under its thumb. This enables it to organize and sway the emotions of the masses, and makes its tool of them.

Yet even this answer does not provide a complete solution. Another question arises from it: How is it that these devices succeed so well in rousing men to such wild enthusiasm, even to sacrifice their lives? Only one answer is possible. Because man has within him a lust for hatred and destruction. In normal times this passion exists in a latent state, it emerges only in unusual circumstances; but it is a comparatively easy task to call it into play and raise it to the power of a collective psychosis. Here lies, perhaps, the crux of all the complex factors we are considering, an enigma that only the expert in the lore of human instincts can resolve.

And so we come to our last question. Is it possible to control man's mental evolution so as to make him proof against the psychosis of hate and destructiveness? Here I am thinking by no means only of the so-called uncultured masses. Experience proves that it is rather the so-called "intelligentsia" that is most apt to yield to these disastrous collective suggestions, since the intellectual has no direct contact with life in the raw but encounters it in its easiest, synthetic form–upon the printed page.

To conclude: I have so far been speaking only of wars between nations; what are known as international conflicts. But I am well aware that the aggressive instinct operates under other forms and in other circumstances. (I am thinking of civil wars, for instance, due in earlier days to religious zeal, but nowadays to social factors; or, again, the persecution of racial minorities.) But my insistence on what is the most typical, most cruel and extravagant form of conflict between man and man was deliberate, for here we have the best occasion of discovering ways and means to render all armed conflicts impossible.

I know that in your writings we may find answers,[2] explicit or implied, to all the issues of this urgent and absorbing problem. But it would be of the greatest service to us all were you to present the problem of world peace in the light of your most recent discoveries, for such a presentation well might blaze the trail for new and fruitful modes of action.

Yours very sincerely,

Albert Einstein

---

2 Freud had penned a lengthy reply to Einstein's letter. Systematically delineating the history of war from the stone age to the present, he had surmised that war came instinctually to man whenever there was a conflict of desires among people. According to him, there is no permanent solution to prevent a war.

Clever and Patriotic Womenfolk

Albert Einstein's open letter to New York Times

3rd December, 1932

Never yet have I experienced from the fair sex such energetic rejection of all advances;[1] or, if I have, never from so many at once.

But are they not quite right, these watchful citizenesses? Why should one open one's doors to a person who devours hard-boiled capitalists with as much appetite and gusto as the Cretan Minotaur in days gone by devoured luscious Greek maidens, and on top of that is low-down enough to reject every sort of war, except the unavoidable war with one's own wife? Therefore give heed to

---

1 The President of the Woman Patriot Corporation, Mrs. Randolph Frothingam sent a letter to the US immigration authorities, demanding that Einstein should be deported, labelling him as 'powerful' and 'dangerous' since she was convinced that he was both an anarchist and a communist. Her views were supported by other women in the Corporation.

your clever and patriotic womenfolk and remember that the Capitol of mighty Rome was once saved by the cackling of its faithful geese.

Albert Einstein

Things to Worry and Not Worry About

Francis Scott Fitzgerald's[1] letter to Frances Scott Fitzgerald

La Paix, Rodgers' Forge
Towson, Maryland

August 8, 1933

Dear Pie:[2]

I feel very strongly about you doing duty. Would you give me a little more documentation about your reading in French? I am glad you are happy — but I never believe much in happiness. I never believe in misery either. Those are things you see on the stage or the screen or the printed pages, they never really happen to you in life.

---

1 Author of the acclaimed novel, *The Great Gatsby.*

2 Pie was the nickname given to Francis Scott Fitzgerald's only daughter, Frances.

All I believe in in life is the rewards for virtue (according to your talents) and the *punishments* for not fulfilling your duties, which are doubly costly. If there is such a volume in the camp library, will you ask Mrs. Tyson to let you look up a sonnet of Shakespeare's in which the line occurs "*Lillies that fester smell far worse than weeds.*"[3]

Have had no thoughts today, life seems composed of getting up a *Saturday Evening Post* story. I think of you, and always pleasantly; but if you call me "Pappy" again I am going to take the White Cat out and beat his bottom *hard, six times for every time you are impertinent.* Do you react to that?

I will arrange the camp bill.

Halfwit, I will conclude.

Things to worry about:

Worry about courage
Worry about Cleanliness
Worry about efficiency
Worry about horsemanship
Worry about. . .

---

3 This line occurs in Sonnet 94 of *Shakespeare's Sonnets.*

Things not to worry about:

Don't worry about popular opinion
Don't worry about dolls
Don't worry about the past
Don't worry about the future
Don't worry about growing up
Don't worry about anybody getting ahead of you
Don't worry about triumph
Don't worry about failure unless it comes through your own fault
Don't worry about mosquitoes
Don't worry about flies
Don't worry about insects in general
Don't worry about parents
Don't worry about boys
Don't worry about disappointments[4]
Don't worry about pleasures
Don't worry about satisfactions

---

4 Fitzgerald wrote this letter to his daughter when she was thirteen years old. He asked her not to worry about disappointing others, perhaps remembering his own childhood. He had struggled to pass in school, and was known to cut class at Princeton University as well, something that must have bothered his own parents. Regardless, he dropped out and joined the military.

Things to think about:

What am I really aiming at?
How good am I really in comparison to my contemporaries[5] in regard to:

(a) Scholarship
(b) Do I really understand about people and am I able to get along with them?
(c) Am I trying to make my body a useful instrument or am I neglecting it?

With dearest love,

Daddy

P.S. My come-back to your calling me Pappy is christening you by the word Egg, which implies that you belong to a very rudimentary state of life and that I could break you up and crack you open at my will and I think it would be a word that would hang on if I ever told it to your contemporaries. "Egg Fitzgerald." How would you like that to go through life with — "Eggie Fitzgerald" or

5 One of these contemporaries, that Fitzgerald might have been comparing himself to, was Ernest Hemingway. They were friends turned foes. Hemingway had nursed a dislike to Fitzgerald's wife, and had even derided his work on many occasions. By the late 1920s, their friendship had all but come to an end.

"Bad Egg Fitzgerald" or any form that might occur to fertile minds? Try it once more and I swear to God I will hang it on you and it will be up to you to shake it off. Why borrow trouble?

Love anyhow.

It Is Nothing to Be Ashamed of

Sigmund Freud's letter to a mother

April 9th 1935

Dear Mrs. [the name was erased]

I gather from your letter that your son is a homosexual. I am most impressed by the fact, that you do not mention this term yourself in your information about him. May I question you why you avoid it? Homosexuality is assuredly no advantage, but it is nothing to be ashamed of, no vice, no degradation, it cannot be classified as an illness; we consider it to be a variation of the sexual function produced by a certain arrest of sexual development.[1] Many highly respectable individuals of ancient and modern times have been homosexuals, several of the greatest men

1 Freud's theory was that people were born bisexual, and chose to be straight or gay observing, or being influenced by, the people in their lives.

among them[2] (Plato, Michelangelo, Leonardo da Vinci, etc.) It is a great injustice to persecute homosexuality as a crime and cruelty too.[3] If you do not believe me, read the books of Havelock Ellis.

By asking me if I can help, you mean, I suppose, if I can abolish homosexuality and make normal heterosexuality take its place. The answer is, in a general way, we cannot promise to achieve this. In a certain number of cases we succeed in developing the blighted germs of heterosexual tendencies, which are present in every homosexual;[4] in the majority of cases it is no longer possible. It is a question of the quality and the age of the individual. The result of treatment cannot be predicted.

What analysis can do for your son runs in a different line. If he is unhappy, neurotic, torn by conflicts, inhibited in

---

2 In an interview with a correspondent from the Vienna newspaper *Die Zeit*, Freud had said 'I advocate the standpoint that the homosexual does not belong before the tribunal of a court of law. I am even of the firm conviction that homosexuals must not be treated as sick people, for a perverse orientation is far from being a sickness. Wouldn't that oblige us to characterize as sick many great thinkers and scholars whom we admire precisely because of their mental health?'

3 In the early 20th century, the social intolerance of homosexuality bordered on considering it an illness, an abnormality.

4 Normal heterosexual function required a sublimated homosexuality, and all homosexuals had some heterosexual feelings, according to Freud.

his social life, analysis may bring him harmony, peace of mind, full efficiency, whether he remains a homosexual or gets changed. If you make up your mind he should have analysis with me—I don't expect you will—, he has to come over to Vienna. I have no intention of leaving here. However, don't neglect to give me your answer.

Sincerely yours with best wishes,

Freud

P.S.

I did not find it difficult to read your handwriting. Hope you will not find my writing and my English a harder task.

Some Spirit is Manifest in the Laws of the Universe

Albert Einstein's letter to Phyllis

January 24, 1936

Dear Phyllis,

I will attempt to reply to your question[1] as simply as I can. Here is my answer:

Scientists believe that every occurrence, including the affairs of human beings, is due to the laws of nature. Therefore a scientist cannot be inclined to believe that the course of events can be influenced by prayer, that is, by a supernaturally manifested wish.

However, we must concede that our actual knowledge of these forces is imperfect, so that in the end the belief in the existence of a final, ultimate spirit rests on a kind of faith. Such belief

---

1 A young girl, Phyllis, had written a letter to Einstein, asking him 'do scientists pray and what do they pray for.'

remains widespread even with the current achievements in science.

But also, everyone who is seriously involved in the pursuit of science becomes convinced that some spirit is manifest in the laws of the universe, one that is vastly superior to that of man. In this way the pursuit of science leads to a religious feeling of a special sort, which is surely quite different from the religiosity of someone more naive.

With cordial greetings,

your A. Einstein

I Smell Violence in the Air

M K Gandhi's letter to Subhash Chandra Bose

Birla House,

New Delhi,

2-4-1939

MY DEAR SUBHASH,

I have yours of 31st March as also the previous one. You are quite frank and I like your letters for the clear enunciation of your views.

The views you express seem to me to be so diametrically opposed to those of the others and my own that I do not see any possibility of bridging them.[1] I think that such school of thought should be able to put forth its views before the country without any mixture. And

---

1 India's struggle for independence saw a divide in the political activists into Moderates and Extremists. Moderates, like Gandhi, believed in non-violent means to gain independence, whereas Extremists, like Bose, propagated that non-violence would not be enough, that blood would be inevitably spilled in the freedom struggle.

if this is honestly done, I do not see why there should be any bitterness ending in civil war.

What is wrong is not the differences between us but loss of mutual respect and trust. This will be remedied by time which is the best healer. If there is real non-violence in us, there can be no civil war much less bitterness.

Taking all things into consideration, I am of opinion that you should at once form your own Cabinet fully representing your views. Formulate your programme definitely and put it before the forthcoming A.I.C.C.[2] If the Committee accepts the programme all will be plain- sailing and you should be enabled to prosecute it unhampered by the minority. If on the other hand your programme is not accepted you should resign and let the Committee choose its President. And you will be free to educate the country along your own lines. I tender this advice irrespective of Pandit Pant's resolution.

My prestige does not count. It has an independent value of its own. When my motive is suspected or my policy or programme rejected by the country, the prestige must go. India will rise and fall by the quality of the sum-total of her many millions. Individuals, however high they may be, are of no account except in so far as they represent the many millions. Therefore let us rule it out of consideration.

---

2 All India Congress Committee.

I wholly dissent from your view that the country has been never so non-violent as now. I smell violence in the air I breath. But the violence has put on a subtle form. Our mutual I wholly dissent from your view that the country has been never so non-violent as now. I smell violence in the air I breath. But the violence has put on a subtle form. Our mutual distrust is a bad form of violence. The widening gulf between Hindus and Mussalmans points to the same thing.[3] I can give further illustrations.

We seem to differ as to the amount of corruption in the Congress. My impression is that it is on the increase. I have been pleading for the past many months for a thorough scrutiny.

In these circumstances I see no atmosphere of non-violent mass action. An ultimatum without effective sanction is worse than useless.

But as I have told you I am an old man perhaps growing timid and over-cautious and you have youth before you and reckless optimism born of youth. I hope you are right. I am wrong. I have the firm belief that the Congress as it is today cannot deliver the goods, cannot offer civil disobedience worth the name. Therefore if your

---

3 The already existing antagonism between the two major religious communities was fuelled further by the British government's efforts to 'divide and conquer'.

prognosis is right, I am a back number and played out as the generalissimo of Satyagraha.

I am glad you have mentioned the little Rajkot affair. It brings into prominent relief the different angles from which we look at things. I have nothing to repent of in the steps I have taken in connection with it. I feel that it has great national importance. I have not stopped civil disobedience in the other States for the sake of Rajkot. But Rajkot opened my eyes. It showed me the way. I am not in Delhi for my health. I am reluctantly in Delhi awaiting the Chief Justice's decision. I hold it to be my duty to be in Delhi till the steps to be taken in due fulfilment of the Viceroy's declaration in his last wire to me are finally taken. I may not run any risk. If I invited the Paramount Power to do its duty, I was bound to be in Delhi to see that the duty was fully performed. I saw nothing wrong in the Chief Justice being appointed the interpreter of the document whose meaning was put in doubt by the Thakor Sahib. By the way, Sir Maurice will examine the document not in his capacity as Chief Justice but as a trained jurist trusted by the Viceroy. By accepting the Viceroy's nominee as Judge, I fancy I have shown both wisdom and grace and what is more important I have increased the Viceregal responsibility in the matter.

Though we have discussed sharp differences of opinion between us, I am quite sure that our private relations will not suffer in the least. If they are from the heart, as I believe they are, they will bear the strain of these differences.

Love,
BAPU

For the Sake of Humanity

M K Gandhi's letter[1] to Adolf Hitler

As at Wardha,
C. P.,
23-7-'39

Dear friend,

Friends have been urging me to write to you for the sake of humanity. But I have resisted their request, because of the feeling that any letter from me would be an impertinence. Something tells me that I must not calculate and that I must make my appeal for whatever it may be worth.

It is quite clear that you are today the one person in the world who can prevent a war[2] which may reduce humanity to a savage state. Must

---

1 Hitler never read this letter since he did not receive it. The British, who had colonized India at the time, intercepted the letter midway.

2 Gandhi is referring to the Second World War which began in 1939, when German forces invaded Poland.

you pay that price for an object however worthy it may appear to you to be? Will you listen to the appeal of one who has deliberately shunned the method of war not without considerable success? Any way I anticipate your forgiveness, if I have erred in writing to you.

I remain,

Your sincere friend

M. K. Gandhi

HERR HITLER
BERLIN
GERMANY.

To Set Up a Nuclear Chain Reaction

Albert Einstein's letter to Franklin Roosevelt

Albert Einstein
Old Grove Rd.
Nassau Point
Peconic, Long Island

August 2nd, 1939

F.D. Roosevelt,
President of the United States,
White House
Washington, D.C.

Sir:

Some recent work by E. Fermi and L. Szilard, which has been communicated to me in manuscript, leads me to expect that the element uranium may be turned into a new and important source of energy in the immediate future. Certain aspects of the situation which has arisen seem to call for watchfulness and, if necessary, quick action on the part of the Administration.[1] I believe therefore that it is my duty to bring to your attention the following facts and recommendations:

In the course of the last four months it has been made probable - through the work of Joliot in France as well as Fermi and Szilard in America - that it may become possible to set up a nuclear chain reaction in a large mass of uranium, by which vast amounts of power and large quantities of new radium-like elements would be generated. Now it appears almost certain that this could be achieved in the immediate future.

This new phenomenon would also lead to the construction of bombs, and it is conceivable - though much less certain - that extremely powerful bombs of a new type may thus be constructed. A single bomb of this type, carried by boat and exploded in a port, might very well destroy the whole port together with some of the surrounding territory. However, such bombs might very well prove to be too heavy for transportation by air.

---

1 The Second World War had started that year. Einstein was concerned that Hitler might be planning to drop a nuclear bomb. Indeed, Germany's secret program, Uranverein or 'Uranium Club' had started in April 1939.

The United States has only very poor ores of uranium in moderate quantities. There is some good ore in Canada and the former Czechoslovakia, while the most important source of uranium is Belgian Congo.

In view of the situation you may think it desirable to have some permanent contact maintained between the Administration and the group of physicists working on chain reactions in America. One possible way of achieving this might be for you to entrust with this task a person[2] who has your confidence and who could perhaps serve in an inofficial capacity. His task might comprise the following:

a) to approach Government Departments, keep them informed of the further development, and put forward recommendations for Government action, giving particular attention to the problem of securing a supply of uranium ore for the United States;
b) to speed up the experimental work, which is at present being carried on within the limits of the budgets of University laboratories, by providing funds, if such

---

2 Einstein's letter had the desired effect on the President. He showed it to his military adviser, and consequently the Manhattan Project was started. Led by the United States, and supported by the United Kingdom and Canada, its aim was to develop an atomic weapon before the German forces did.

funds be required, through his contacts with private persons who are willing to make contributions for this cause, and perhaps also by obtaining the co-operation of industrial laboratories which have the necessary equipment.

I understand that Germany has actually stopped the sale of uranium from the Czechoslovakian mines which she has taken over. That she should have taken such early action might perhaps be understood on the ground that the son of the German Under-Secretary of State, von Weizsäcker, is attached to the Kaiser-Wilhelm-Institut in Berlin where some of the American work on uranium is now being repeated.

Yours very truly,

(Signed)

(Albert Einstein)

Keep Me in Touch

Franklin Roosevelt's letter to Winston Churchill, dated 11 September 1939

My dear Churchill,

It is because you and I occupied similar positions[1] in the World War that I want you to know how glad I am that you are back again in the Admiralty. Your problems are, I realise, complicated by new factors but the essential is not very different. What I want you and the Prime Minister to know is that I shall at all times welcome it if you will keep me in touch personally with anything you want me to know about.[2] You can always send sealed letters through your pouch or my pouch. I am glad you did the Marlboro volumes[3] before

---

1 Franklin Roosevelt had been the assistant secretary of the US Navy when he first met Winston Churchill in 1918, at the time of the First World War.

2 This offer of help was appreciated by Churchill, who presented this letter to the War Cabinet.

3 Winston Churchill wrote *Marlborough: His Life and Times* in four volumes. The book was about John Churchill, the first duke of Marlborough.

this thing[4] started – and I have much enjoyed reading them.

With my sincere regards,

Faithfully yours,

FRANKLIN D. ROOSEVELT

---

4 The Second World War.

To Change Thanksgiving Day

A common man's letter to Franklin Roosevelt

Shinnston, W. Va.
August 15, 1939

The President
White House
Washington, D.C.

Mr. President:

I see by the paper this morning where you want to change Thanksgiving Day to November 23[1] of which I heartily approve. Thanks.

---

1 During the final years of the Great Depression, Roosevelt preponed Thanksgiving a week to stretch the Christmas shopping season in order to improve the retail sales. This evinced a mixed response from the citizens of America. Some of whom lauded it as an excellent move while others were skeptical about how much it would help alleviating the country's economy. One of the letters Roosevelt received after this announcement, claimed that Roosevelt had lost his popularity and goodwill after this.

Now, there are some things that I would like done and would appreciate your approval:

1. Have Sunday changed to Wednesday;

2. Have Monday's to be Christmas;

3. Have it strictly against the Will of God to work on Tuesday;

4. Have Thursday to be Pay Day with time and one-half for overtime;

5. Require everyone to take Friday and Saturday off for a fishing trip down the Potomac.

With these in view and hoping you will give me some consideration at your next Congress, I remain,

Yours very truly

(Signed)

Shelby O. Bennett

My Good Friend Roosvelt

Fidel Castro's letter to Franklin Roosevelt

Santiago de Cuba

Nov 6 1940

Mr Franklin Roosvelt, President of the United States.

My good friend Roosvelt I don't know very English, but I know as much as write to you. I like to hear the radio, and I am very happy, because I heard in it, that you will be President for a new (periodo). I am twelve years old.[1] I am a boy but I think very much but I do not think that I am writing to the President of the United States. If you like, give me a ten dollars bill green american, in the letter, because never, I have not

---

1 When he was twenty-four, Fidel Castro led the historic Cuban revolution that overthrew the dictatorship of Fulgencio Batista, and paved the way for him to become Cuba's Prime Minister.

seen a ten dollars bill green american and I would like to have one of them.

My address is:

Sr Fidel Castro
Colegio de Dolores
Santiago de Cuba
Oriente Cuba

I don't know very English but I know very much Spanish and I suppose you don't know very Spanish but you know very English because you are American but I am not American.

(Thank you very much)

Good by. Your friend,

[Signed]

Fidel Castro

If you want iron to make your ~~sheaps~~ ships I will show to you the bigest (minas) of iron of the land. They are in Mayari Oriente Cuba.

I Am Going Mad Again

Virginia Woolf's letter to Leonard Woolf, written c. 1941

Tuesday.

Dearest,

I feel certain that I am going mad again.[1] I feel we can't go through another of those terrible times. And I shan't recover this time. I begin to hear voices, and I can't concentrate.[2] So I am doing what seems the best thing to do. You have given me the greatest possible happiness. You have been in every way all that anyone could be. I don't think two people could have been happier

---

1 Virginia Woolf had her first breakdown when she was thirteen and her mental illness plagued her throughout the rest of her life. Her husband reported how Virginia had manic episodes, when she would talk incessantly, and how she would have bouts of depression and mood swings.

2 Woolf's mental illness had given shape to many of her characters, one of them being Septimus Smith, in *Mrs. Dalloway*. He too, like Woolf, was plagued by hallucinations, and heard voices of the dead after serving in the war.

till this terrible disease came. I can't fight any longer.[3] I know that I am spoiling your life, that without me you could work. And you will I know. You see I can't even write this properly. I can't read. What I want to say is I owe all the happiness of my life to you. You have been entirely patient with me and incredibly good. I want to say that — everybody knows it. If anybody could have saved me it would have been you.[4] Everything has gone from me but the certainty of your goodness. I can't go on spoiling your life any longer.

I don't think two people could have been happier than we have been.

V.

---

3 This letter was discovered by Leonard Woolf on the day Virginia killed herself.

4 The day before her suicide, Leonard had taken Virginia to consult a doctor but Virginia had lost all hope, refusing to be treated. The next morning, she stuffed rocks in her pockets and drowned herself in the sea.

I Have Long Been Trying to Be a Fakir

M K Gandhi's letter to Winston Churchill

Dilkusha,

Panchagani,

17th July 1944

Dear Prime Minister,

You are reported to have the desire to crush the simple 'naked fakir',[1] as you are said to have described me. I have been long trying to be a fakir and that naked—a more difficult task. I, therefore, regard the expression as a compliment though unintended. I approach you then as such and ask you to trust and use me for the sake of your people and mine and through them those of the world.

Your sincere friend,
M. K. GANDHI

---

1 The United Kingdom's Prime Minister, Winston Churchill, had called Gandhi a 'naked fakir', saying that he was disappointed that Gandhi didn't die on his hunger strike.

Chakravarti Rajagopalachari had advised Gandhi against sending this letter. The letter reached Churchill after three months.

I Am Not Pleased with the Book

George Orwell's letter to Frederic Warburg

Barnhill
Isle of Jura
Argyllshire
22.10.48

Dear Fred,[1]

You will have had my wire by now, and if anything crossed your mind I dare say I shall have had a return wire from you by the time this goes off. I shall finish the book, D.V., early in November, and I am rather flinching from the job of typing it, because it is a very awkward thing to do in bed, where I still have to spend half the time. Also there will have to be carbon copies, a thing which always fidgets me, and the

1 Fredric Warburg was George Orwell's publisher. Orwell's critically acclaimed *Animal Farm* had been rejected by many publishing houses, till Warburg decided to publish it.

book is fearfully long, I should think well over 100,000 words, possibly 125,000. I can't send it away because it is an unbelievably bad MS and no one could make head or tail of it without explanation. On the other hand a skilled typist under my eye could do it easily enough. If you can think of anybody who would be willing to come, I will send money for the journey and full instructions. I think we could make her quite comfortable. There is always plenty to eat and I will see that she has a comfortable warm place to work in.

I am not pleased with the book but I am not absolutely dissatisfied. I first thought of it in 1943. I think it is a good idea but the execution would have been better if I had not written it under the influence of TB.[2] I haven't definitely fixed on the title but I am hesitating between NINETEEN EIGHTY-FOUR and THE LAST MAN IN EUROPE.[3]

---

2 George Orwell died from TB in 1950.

3 The title that Orwell went with was '1984', and the book was published a year after Orwell sent this letter, on 8 June 1949.

I have just had Sartre's book on antisemitism,[4] which you published, to review. I think Sartre is a bag of wind and I am going to give him a good boot.

Please give everyone my love.

Yours

(Signed, 'George')

---

4 George Orwell published a review of Jean-Paul Sarte's *Portrait of the Antisemite*, which ran in *The Observer*.

Your End Is Approaching

FBI's letter to Martin Luther King Jr., dated November 1964

KING,

In view of your low grade, abnormal personal behavior I[1] will not dignify your name with either a Mr. or a Reverend or a Dr. And, your last name calls to mind only the type of King such as King Henry the VIII and his countless acts of adultery and immoral conduct lower than that of a beast.

King, look into your heart. You know you are a complete fraud[2] and a great liability to all of us Negroes. White people in this country have enough frauds of their own but I am sure they don't have one at this time that is any where

---

1 This letter has occupied a unique place in the history of American intelligence. Though the name of the exact sender is not known, people suspect it to be the then FBI director, John Edgar Hoover.

2 Hoover had called King 'the most notorious liar in the country' at a news conference that year.

near your equal. You are no clergyman and you know it. I repeat you are a colossal fraud and an evil, vicious one at that. You could not believe in God and act as you do. Clearly you don't believe in any personal moral principles.

King, like all frauds your end is approaching. You could have been our greatest leader. You, even at an early age have turned out to be not a leader but a dissolute, abnormal moral imbecile. We will now have to depend on our older leaders like Wilkins a man of character and thank God we have others like him. But you are done. Your "honorary" degrees, your Nobel Prize (what a grim farce) and other awards will not save you. King, I repeat you are done.

No person can overcome facts, not even a fraud like yourself. Lend your sexually psychotic ear to the enclosure. You will find yourself and in all your dirt, filth, evil and moronic talk exposed on the record for all time.[3] I repeat — no person can argue successfully against facts. You are finished. You will find on the record for all time your filthy, dirty, evil companions, male and females giving expression with you to your hidious abnormalities. And some of them to pretend to be ministers of the Gospel.

---

3 A year before this letter was written, Attorney General, Robert Kennedy had approved wiretapping of King's phones.

Satan could not do more. What incredible evilness. It is all there on the record, your sexual orgies. Listen to yourself you filthy, abnormal animal. You are on the record. You have been on the record — all your adulterous acts, your sexual orgies extending far into the past. This one is but a tiny sample. You will understand this. Yes, from your various evil playmates on the east coast to [redacted] and others on the west coast and outside the country you are on the record. King you are done.

The American public, the church organizations that have been helping — Protestant, Catholic and Jews will know you for what you are — an evil, abnormal beast. So will others who have backed you. You are done.

King, there is only one thing left for you to do. You know what it is. You have just 34 days in which to do (this exact number has been selected for a specific reason, it has definite practical significant. You are done. There is but one way out for you. You better take it before your filthy, abnormal fraudulent self is bared to the nation.[4]

4 Martin Luther King Jr. was assassinated four years later.

In the Event of Moon Disaster

H. R. Haldeman's letter to Bill Safire

To: H. R. Haldeman[1]
From: Bill Safire

July 18, 1969.

IN EVENT OF MOON DISASTER:

Fate has ordained that the men who went to the moon to explore in peace will stay on the moon to rest in peace.[2]

These brave men, Neil Armstrong and Edwin Aldrin, know that there is no hope for their recovery. But they also know that there is hope for mankind in their sacrifice.

---

1 Richard Nixon's Chief of Staff.

2 For the first time in history, men were going to land on moon. This speech was prepared in case things went sideways, and Neil Armstrong and Buzz Aldrin died during the mission. Fortunately, this didn't happen and hence, this speech was never delivered.

These two men are laying down their lives in mankind's most noble goal: the search for truth and understanding.

They will be mourned by their families and friends; they will be mourned by the nation; they will be mourned by the people of the world; they will be mourned by a Mother Earth that dared send two of her sons into the unknown.

In their exploration, they stirred the people of the world to feel as one; in their sacrifice, they bind more tightly the brotherhood of man.

In ancient days, men looked at the stars and saw their heroes in the constellations. In modern times, we do much the same, but our heroes are epic men of flesh and blood.

Others will follow, and surely find their way home. Man's search will not be denied. But these men were the first, and they will remain the foremost in our hearts.

For every human being who looks up at the moon in the nights to come will know that there is some corner of another world that is forever mankind.

PRIOR TO THE PRESIDENT'S STATEMENT:

The President should telephone each of the widows-to-be.

AFTER THE PRESIDENT'S STATEMENT, AT THE POINT WHEN NASA ENDS COMMUNICATIONS WITH THE MEN:

A clergyman should adopt the same procedure as a burial at sea, commending their souls to "the deepest of the deep," concluding with the Lord's Prayer.

All I Need Is the Federal Credentials

Elvis Presley's letter to Richard Nixon, dated 1970

Dear Mr President,

First, I would like to introduce myself. I am Elvis Presley and admire you and have great respect for your office. I talked to vice-president Agnew in Palm Springs three weeks ago and expressed my concerns for our country. The drug culture, the hippie elements, the SDS, Black Panthers, etc do not consider me as their enemy or as they call it, the establishment. I call it America and I love it. Sir, I can and will be of any service that I can to help the country out. I have no concerns or motives other than helping the country out.

So, I wish not to be given a title or an appointed position. I can and will do more good if I were made a federal agent at large and I will help out by doing it my way through communications with people of all ages. First and foremost, I am an entertainer, but all I need is the federal credentials. I am on the plane with Senator

George Murphy and we have been discussing the problems that our country is faced with.

Sir, I am staying at the Washington hotel, Room 505-506-507. I have two men who work with me by the name of Jerry Schilling and Sonny West. I am registered under the name of Jon Burrows. I will be here for as long as it takes to get the credentials of a federal agent. I have done an in-depth study of drug abuse and communist brainwashing techniques and I am right in the middle of the whole thing, where I can and will do the most good.

I am glad to help just so long as it is kept very private. You can have your staff or whomever call me anytime today, tonight or tomorrow. I was nominated this coming year one of America's 10 most outstanding young men. That will be in January 18 in my home town of Memphis, Tennessee. I am sending you a short autobiography about myself so you can better understand this approach. I would love to meet you just to say hello if you're not too busy.[1]

---

1 Elvis Presley personally delivered this letter at the White House. After dropping off the letter, he went to the Bureau of Narcotics and Dangerous Drugs, to request the badge he so coveted, in case the letter didn't work. His request was not granted. However, when he went back to the White House, a meeting with the President had been arranged for him, who, to Elvis' surprise, gave him the badge.